TELL THEM THAT I LOVE THEM

John DiBattista Jr.

WestBow
PRESS
A DIVISION OF THOMAS NELSON

WestBow Press books may be ordered through booksellers or by contacting:

WestBow Press
A Division of Thomas Nelson
1663 Liberty Drive
Bloomington, IN 47403
www.westbowpress.com
1-(866) 928-1240

ISBN: 978-1-4497-3728-3 (hc)
ISBN: 978-1-4497-3727-6 (sc)
ISBN: 978-1-4497-3726-9 (e)

Library of Congress Control Number: 2012900828

Printed in the United States of America

WestBow Press rev. date: 05/02/2012

DEDICATED TO
BROTHER JOSEPH LOVALVO

Brother Joe was born on March 1, 1910 and passed on to his reward on December 31, 2005. Everyone who knew Brother Joe, even those who did not have extensive interaction with him, would agree that he was a unique man—a man of God.

As I started my spiritual journey, the Holy Spirit directed me to Brother Joe, and he became my mentor for more than fifteen years. He never tired of teaching and demonstrating God's love and power to me.

He had an unquenchable desire to testify of Jesus Christ and the gospel that had been restored and unselfishly passed it on to all who would listen. My words do not sufficiently express my love and respect for this man and how he impacted my life.

TELL THEM THAT I LOVE THEM

Preface

This collection of miraculous, supernatural events has shaped the past sixty years of my life. Fortunately, I am blessed to have a daughter, Christine, who insisted that I keep a journal. To ensure that I did, she gave me one each Christmas for several years.

My wife, Caryl; my son, John; and several of my friends and colleagues have urged me to write these experiences so that others might benefit and be blessed from the hope and encouragement that they bring.

I would like to be able to take some form of credit for these and the many other spiritual experiences that I have enjoyed and am about to share with you, but I can't. I suggest that these types of events are probably happening in many of your lives as well, but no one has stimulated your spiritual sensitivity to the point that you recognize them for what they are—interventions by God. After all, the responsibility of the Holy Spirit is to draw all men and women to Him through the demonstration of His unconditional love.

I hope that when you read these examples of God's grace, you will realize that His love extends to you and want to make Him your Lord and Savior, as I did.

> "For God sent not his Son into the world to condemn the world; but that the world through him might be saved" (John 3:17).

May God bless you.

STATEMENT OF PHILOSOPHY

I t is my firm belief that each of us came into this world with a purpose and that we were given the tools to fulfill that purpose. We were created in God's image and gifted by our Creator to represent Him in some manner, small or great. While we are on our life's journey, our life's true purpose unfolds. I have also discovered that many people are slow to realize their purpose, and in fact, many go to their graves without ever having had the opportunity to live it. These people seem to face death with uneasiness and uncertainty, as the man who received one talent in the parable of the talents experienced (Matthew 25:14-30).

I believe that the rebirthing process allows us to rediscover our individual purpose. Our lives get reoriented through the process of belief, faith, repentance, baptism, and receipt of the Holy Spirit. We regain the opportunity to make our unique contribution to the world. Being born again allows us to grow into the spiritual people we were intended to be, regardless of how flawed we have become.

The process, though, has been so distorted through time that it does not often carry with it the promises intended. The power has been lost as men and institutions have modified or dismissed the original process.

My purpose is to tell all that the power of being born again has not been lost. In fact, when completed as directed and demonstrated by Christ, the recipient will enjoy the promised heavenly blessings while in the flesh. My book, *Tell*

Them That I Love Them, recounts the process and the results enjoyed through a series of short stories.

Contact John at
www.tellthemthatilovethem.net
JohnD@johncaryl.com

CONTENTS

INTRODUCTION

Therefore I say unto you, Take no thought for your
life, what ye shall eat, or what ye shall drink; nor
yet for your body, what ye shall put on. Is not the
life more than meat, and the body than raiment?
Behold the fowls of the air: for they sow not,
neither do they reap, nor gather into barns; yet
your heavenly Father feedeth them. Are ye not
much better than they?

—Matthew 6:25-26

A wet June midnight in 1992 found me and my missionary friend, Joel, standing on a damp platform in *Roma Termini,* exhausted from our long train ride and the past seven days of non-stop church work. We were both mentally worn from attempting to communicate in Italian and almost completely drained of our allotted daily funds. We felt invisible as we stood there, jostled by a thousand other travelers bustling purposefully toward a thousand different destinations. We didn't even know where we would sleep that night. The rain began to come down hard.

In the darkness, a voice asked, "Why don't we pray?" It was as if Joel could read my mind.

"What a novel idea for two missionaries," I responded. Setting down our luggage, we joined hands and offered prayer. It was short and ineloquent, but the words were pure in spirit. "Lord, please send someone to help us. We are here, doing your work, and we need your help. In Jesus' name we pray."

We had picked up our luggage and taken two steps toward the nearest taxi queue when a young man walked up to us and said in perfect English, "I came to help you."

The prayer that had just been so freshly offered didn't register in our minds as we introduced ourselves to this stranger. He responded to our greetings by simply saying, "Hello. My name is Daniel. What can I do for you?"

"We're exhausted, and we don't speak Italian," I explained. "We need food, shelter, and transportation. And we only have 80,000 lire." (That was about $65)

Pulling a cell phone out of his pocket, Daniel negotiated a room for us at the Florida Hotel near the Fountain of Trevi, one of the most popular tourist attractions in Rome. "The rate is 60,000 lire," he said. "The hotel is brand new, and no one has ever slept in the room reserved for you. It's only a couple of blocks away, but you'll never find it in this downpour."

Without waiting for a response from us, he turned and went out into the rain toward the first taxi in the queue and managed to negotiate our ride for 5,000 lire (about five dollars). The cab driver was visibly unhappy. Apparently, he didn't appreciate having to take his taxi out in the storm for a mere 5,000-lire fare.

Daniel returned and told us to place our bags in the trunk but not to expect any help from the driver, since we didn't have the money to tip him. As we walked toward the taxi, I decided I should get Daniel's address to send him a thank-you note. But when I turned, he was nowhere to be found.

The room was nice. In fact, it was the best accommodation we had experienced on our entire seven-day trip. We didn't stand a chance against the queen-size canopy beds with soft, white linens covering thick, fluffy mattresses. Our stomachs were even satisfied with the pizza slices and Cokes we purchased with the little money we had left over. We even got to see the Fountain of Trevi, where people toss coins over their shoulders and wish for miracles.

As I was wiping sleep away from my eyes the next morning, I decided to call home. It was Sunday evening in California, and when my wife, Caryl, answered, she surprised me by anxiously blurting out, "Are you okay?"

"Sure, I'm great. Why?"

"Today at church, during our afternoon meeting, Brother Frank stood up and said, 'John and Joel are in trouble. Let's get on our knees and pray for them.' Then the entire congregation knelt down and asked God to help you. I was afraid something happened."

"No, nothing happened," I said. We changed the subject and continued our conversation.

Amazingly enough, I didn't put all the pieces of this incident together until well after I returned to the

United States. One evening a few months later, I had the opportunity to share some of the highlights of the trip with our congregation in Modesto, California. When I got to the part about Daniel, two women later testified that while I was speaking, they heard a voice say, "Look up!" When they did, they both saw a young man descending in a column of light behind me. He had his hands lifted toward heaven as if he were worshiping, and they heard a voice say, "This is the angel that I sent to help my servants in Italy."

That same evening, my cell phone rang. It was a friend from the Modesto congregation who said that as he and his family were driving home after the meeting, his young son, Brandon, inquired from the back seat, "Who was that man in church tonight?" He reminded Brandon that it was me. "You know Brother John DiBattista. Remember the time we stayed at his house?"

His son repeated, "No, Dad, not him. The smaller man with him. What was his name?"

That in the mouth of two or three witnesses every word may be established. (Matthew 18:16).

The Spirit of God ignited my imagination, and I saw everything happening simultaneously. I saw the church members in California—my wife included—kneeling down to pray during the afternoon church service. The time would have been approximately 3:00 in the afternoon, which means it was midnight in Italy. I saw Joel and me joining hands to pray in the busy train station. I imagined Daniel descending the column of light and landing softly on the platform. Only when my thoughts turned to God's infinite love and tender concern for my welfare did I realize that my imagination couldn't keep up.

PART ONE

GETTING THERE

TRAINED UP

Train up a child in the way he should go: and
when he is old, he will not depart from it.

—Proverbs 22:6

The first miracle in my life happened when I was just two months old. Despite the indisputable fact that I was a boy, my mom and dad took me to church in a little white dress so that my grandfather, an ordained evangelist in his church, could bless me. Although many faiths practice the baptism of little children, my grandfather's church believed in blessing babies instead.

During a regular Sunday church meeting, my grandfather asked my mom and dad to bring me up front. They placed me in his arms, and he prayed intently that God would bless my life. As my grandfather was praying, one of the elderly women saw a person dressed in white appear at his side. This person blessed me a second time. The elderly woman told my mother what she saw, but I didn't hear about it until I was thirty-eight years old. Still, I grew up sensing that there were other forces at work in my life.

. . . .

But Jesus said unto them, They need not depart;
give ye them to eat. And they say unto him, We
have here but five loaves, and two fishes. He said,
Bring them hither to me. And he commanded the
multitude to sit down on the grass, and took the

five loaves, and the two fishes, and looking up to heaven, he blessed, and brake, and gave the loaves to his disciples, and the disciples to the multitude. And they did all eat, and were filled: and they took up of the fragments that remained twelve baskets full. And they that had eaten were about five thousand men, beside women and children. (Matthew 14:16-21)

The second miracle happened on a humid Saturday morning when I was about six years old. I had been "helping" my grandfather with chores around his small Pennsylvania farm. We had just finished our work and retreated to the cool interior of the house when two cars pulled into the driveway. Looking out the window, Grandpap saw that the visitors pouring out of the two vehicles were church members from Ohio. In his excitement to see friends from far away, Grandpap invited them all inside for lunch.

I went to the pantry to see if I could "help" Gram with the food, and to my surprise, I saw her standing in the middle of the kitchen with a plate of rice in her hands, bawling. The rice, topped with a single pork chop, comprised all the leftovers from last night's dinner, and it was all she had to serve her company. I heard Grandpap's footsteps in the hallway, and when he rounded the corner, he took one look at her and asked, "What's the problem?"

"I don't have enough food for our guests," Gram sobbed, embarrassed that she wasn't prepared to give them a proper welcome.

With the practicality of a man, Grandpap said, "Just put everything we have on the table. I'll go to the garden and get everything you'll need for a big salad. It will be fine."

The brothers and sisters—in my grandparents' church, the members referred to one another as *brother* and *sister*—gathered around the kitchen table. Prayer was offered, and lunch began. I sat on the floor nearby, listening to their discussion of how the church in Ohio was growing and how they could see God blessing them. When they had finished socializing, the visitors thanked Grandpap and Gram warmly and then departed.

I went to the pantry to help Gram clean up. There she was again, holding the same plate of food in her hands, crying. I asked, "What's wrong now, Gram?"

"We had one pork chop and about a cup and a half of rice on this plate. Now look at the plate. It's full!"

And it was—full of rice and pork chops. There was more on the plate after the meal than there had been beforehand.

Even though I couldn't consider myself a regular Sunday school attendee, I had managed to hear the story of the loaves and the fishes. My small mind knew that something big had just happened. My grandparents were neither rich nor important in their community. They weren't religious scholars, and they didn't possess any extraordinary spiritual qualities that would court God's special favor. They were ordinary farmers. But God's favor had found them anyway.

At that age, I didn't understand the implications of what happened that day, but many years later, something similar would happen to me in Kenya. That time, I fully recognized it as God's benevolence.

. . . .

I had an uncle who was freshly discharged from the Marine Corps, and I thought he was Hercules. There is nothing that can cultivate the adoration of a seven year-old boy like a gentle giant. My uncle was trim, toned, and covered in muscles that I could only fantasize about one day growing. His standard-issue buzz cut made him look exactly like what I pictured a military man should be. I despaired of ever becoming as cool as he was. Despite his imposing physique, my uncle was gentle, kind, and always the first to lend a hand to others. He claimed every ounce of my admiration.

My clearest memory of him was the night of my eighth birthday. Mom had invited the family to a dinner party in my honor, but my uncle couldn't come, because he had promised to help a friend put up stadium lights at a local football field. He paid me a visit in the early afternoon before leaving to accomplish his chore.

Walking into my room, he squatted next to where I was sitting on the floor. With a playful grin, he extended his two fists and said, "Go ahead. Pick one."

After I tapped the hairy knuckles on his right hand, he turned it over, and I found a few dollars crunched in his palm.

"Pick the other one, too," he said. Again, there were a few more dollars. Laughing, he grabbed me, threw me up in the air, and caught me in his strong arms. We laughed as we said goodbye.

An hour or so later, just as we were getting ready to cut my birthday cake, the phone rang. I saw my father answer it, listen for a few moments, and then begin to cry. That night, my uncle had been electrocuted when a power line broke and fell on him. He had died instantly.

Even though I was just a kid, I resolved that one day, I would be like him and wear the uniform that he so proudly wore. I wanted to be a Marine.

. . . .

"And ye shall teach them, your children,
speaking of them when thou sittest in thine
house, and when thou walkest by the way,
when thou liest down, and when thou risest up."
(Deuteronomy 11:19)

I was fourteen years old, and I had just finished helping Grandpap with his Saturday morning chores.

As I was about to leave, Grandpap motioned for me to sit with him on a little wooden bench just outside the garage for a talk. It's not like Grandpap was always pulling me down on benches for long chats. In fourteen years, he had never done anything like this. *He must have something pretty important to say,* I thought. Maybe he wanted to discuss the changes that were happening to me now that I was becoming more of a man. Maybe he wanted me to take on more responsibility with the farm. My mind went in a thousand different directions, but his topic caught me completely by surprise.

He wanted to talk about the prophecies of God. He began by telling me that God had big plans for the land of America. He said that God had set the Americas apart after the great flood to be an inheritance for the tribe of Joseph, one of the twelve sons of Jacob who God renamed Israel. He spoke of the whole house of Israel—how they had been scattered across the earth and how they would be gathered again by the power of God. He spoke of destruction, peace, and a city called the New Jerusalem that would be built in North America. He said, "Everybody there will be a brother and a friend, and they will wear white garments with gold borders on the sleeves. I won't live to see these things. But you will."

His words sank deep into my mind, or maybe my soul. I couldn't understand much of what he said, but I knew it was important. Grandpap wasn't normally a storyteller, so I knew enough to listen closely. His face seemed to almost shine as he sat on that wooden bench with his elbows on his knees and his neck craned sideways so his eyes could look straight into mine. I wish I could remember the exact words he said. All that remains is the message. What I couldn't possibly know was that this message would someday become the axis upon which my whole life would revolve.

. . . .

"Therefore shall a man leave his father and his mother, and shall cleave unto his wife: and they shall be one flesh." (Genesis 2:24)

It was one of those beautiful Indian summer days in Pennsylvania. I sat staring out the window of my homeroom, wishing that I was at the lake with my fishing pole or on the football field instead of cooped up in a classroom. As I was daydreaming, the door opened, and a girl walked in and handed my teacher a slip of paper from the front office. I can't describe what happened next except to say that I heard an audible voice speak these words: "This is the wife I have selected for you."

I sat in disbelief for a few moments. I knew the girl. She was Caryl King. I had often sat next to her in study hall. I would annoy her until we both got in trouble. But I had never thought about marrying her. I hadn't thought about marrying anyone. I was just a kid. I didn't even understand the full meaning of what I had just heard.

Caryl and I were married shortly after high school graduation. Forty-two years, two children, three grandchildren, eighteen homes, and eight states later, I love her more today than I did the day she became my wife.

It's funny sometimes how the events in our lives make us read Scripture differently. The situation we're in at the moment shifts our perspective, and we read the same old thing in a brand new way. People often say, "You can read this chapter twenty different times and learn twenty different lessons from it." I must agree with them, although I couldn't really understand this phenomenon until it happened to me with Mark 10:9. This verse is a classic marriage Scripture you would expect to hear read at any traditional Christian wedding. "What therefore God hath joined together, let not man put asunder."

I had always thought this verse simply meant, "Don't get divorced." Thankfully, I am able to think a little deeper than I did in high school. I now realize that this Scripture, in addition to discouraging separation, emphasizes the selection process involved in marriage more than the actual marriage vows themselves. It basically promises that God will select your mate for you. "What God hath joined together . . ." I have no doubt that God selected Caryl for me. Denying that God picked her to be my wife would be the same as denying the audible voice I heard that day in my homeroom. To ever separate from her would be like handing a beautifully wrapped gift back to God, saying, "Thanks, but you didn't pick out the right one for me. I'm going to try choosing on my own."

I will always be thankful that the Lord chose my spouse for me. I don't want to think of what might have happened if the decision had been left up to me. After forty-two years of marriage, I have the luxury of looking back and stating confidently, "God knew what He was doing." But when I was in the thick of it, navigating through periods of adjustment and uncertainty, it helped to have a little something extra to which I could attach my certainty. By this, I mean that we sometimes discover funny little coincidences that are just too perfect not to take somewhat seriously.

For Caryl and me, our funny little coincidence was the fact that we had the same spiritual heritage. Caryl's great,

great, great-grandfather came to America from England in the 1850s and found The Church of Jesus Christ in West Elizabeth, Pennsylvania. After a few visits, he was baptized. He eventually became a minister and was later ordained an apostle. (The Church of Jesus Christ patterns its organization after the church that Jesus set up during His ministry. This includes having twelve apostles and seventy evangelists.) He even served as president of The Church of Jesus Christ for many years.

My Grandpap emigrated from Pescara, Italy in 1919. His friends introduced him to The Church of Jesus Christ in Glassport, Pennsylvania, and during his first visit, he felt the Spirit of God, repented of his sins, and asked for his baptism. He was eventually called to be a minister and then an evangelist.

To put this in perspective, The Church of Jesus Christ had about two thousand members from sea to shining sea in the 1960s. The probability that both Caryl and I would share the same spiritual roots is incredibly low. While this didn't mean much to us when we were newlyweds, we later realized that being on the same spiritual playing field made all the difference in our marriage. We also recognize that undeserved blessings fell upon us from the prayers of our predecessors.

A NORMAL LIFE

Before I knew it, I was married with two children. I was also going to school and working two jobs. Life certainly had me spinning my wheels. Even though I was caught up in the day-to-day, I still remembered my uncle, the marine, and having a military career was still one of my life's ambitions. So in November of 1971, I walked into the recruiter's office and took the test to become a Marine Aviator. A few days later, I enlisted.

. . . .

"And the prayer of faith shall save the sick, and the Lord shall raise him up; and if he have committed sins, they shall be forgiven him." (James 5:15)

Boot camp was difficult for almost everybody, but it was especially difficult for someone like me who had to compete with men fresh out of college. Many were athletes and unmarried, not to mention three years younger than me. I was not in the best of shape, and I knew that I would have to work harder than them if I were to make it through thirteen grueling weeks of Officer Candidates School.

When we reached week six, about 30 percent of the candidates had already *dropped on request* and were placed in Casual Company, where they waited for their releases and returns to civilian life. The rest of us were starting to look like Marines, and we were feeling pretty good about ourselves. At that point, I had my accident.

I was first in line to run the obstacle course one morning. Our whole platoon was decked out in boots and utes (utilities), which meant I was carrying a few extra pounds of weight as I maneuvered over the poles and metal bars, which were slick with morning dew. At one point in the course, I lost my footing on the wet metal bars. I fell hard, and I knew that I was seriously hurt. But I kept going.

I managed to make it to the last challenge on the course, which was a forty-foot rope climb. After what seemed like a week, I reached the top. Sliding down, I began to relax—and that's when I could finally feel a searing and nauseating pain grip my body. I became lightheaded, and when I reached the ground, I passed out cold.

I awoke in the military hospital, and the attending physician confirmed the severity of my injury. He said, "They'll be sending you home."

Whether it was from the shock of hearing those words or from the pain medication they had given me, I groaned and twisted between the scratchy white sheets and began floating in and out of sleep for several hours. All I could think about was that I would never wear dress blues. I would never fly an A-4. I would never wear the insignia of a Marine Corp officer.

Around 6:00 that evening, I heard a slight commotion in the entrance of the sick bay and saw my drill sergeant, an intimidating man named Staff Sergeant Bob Calderwood, stalking toward my bed. He barked, "DiBattista, do you want to be a Marine officer?"

"Yes," I replied, "but they told me they are sending me home and that I am not physically qualified to continue."

"Listen to me," he ordered. "*You* have a choice to make. Get out of bed and come back to training, or go home and feel sorry for yourself the rest of your life. It's *your* choice, not theirs."

Baffled, I tried to open my eyes wider so that I could discern if my imagination had fabricated the words I had just heard. The corpsmen who had gathered to watch the scene began to protest when they saw me trying to get out of bed. Sergeant Calderwood did what he did best—scared them with his bark. Then he placed his arm under mine and helped me hobble back to the barracks.

The next six weeks were some of the toughest of my life. Filled with pain and racked by discomfort, I miraculously finished boot camp. But when my wife, parents, and in-laws finally pinned those gold bars on my collars, shoulders, and cover, I knew that I would look at life's future challenges with an entirely new perspective. Little did I know that I was being refined for a greater calling in a very different service—the army of the Lord God Almighty.

"Behold, I have refined thee, but not with silver;
I have chosen thee in the furnace of affliction"
(Isaiah 48:10).

. . . .

"And all things, whatsoever ye shall ask in prayer, believing, ye shall receive." (Matthew 21:22)

After receiving my commission, I attended infantry school for six months. Then I moved Caryl and the kids to Pensacola, Florida, where I attended primary flight school. After successfully learning to solo the T-34, I transitioned to advanced prop and flew the T-28.

If you had asked me, I would have said life was a dream. We had great housing, the money was good, and the camaraderie kept our house full of friends. We were having fun. Caryl and I were in shape and active with the kids. We would run together every day, and in the evening, take the kids to a function on base. Caryl kept busy playing tennis, volunteering at the kids' school, and socializing at the officers' wives club.

This good time—like all superficial good times—did not last long. While stationed in Pensacola, Florida, Caryl grew suddenly ill. She was quickly diagnosed with rheumatoid arthritis and lupus. Her doctors placed her on very strong medicine with harsh side effects. As the disease progressed, I saw her weakening. My heart broke for her. She slept with splints on her arms, and we took her to the warm shower every morning just to get her body's circulation going. The prognosis was that she would become incapacitated within six to eight weeks.

One night, I lay in bed, tossing and turning as I listened to Caryl struggling in her sleep. I was torturing myself with "what ifs," and a million nagging fears were threatening to pull my brain apart. When I saw how feeble Caryl was and remembered how fit and active she had been, my heart swelled with disappointment and anger. Why should she have to suffer when so many other women got to live normal lives?

Without anywhere else to turn, I slid quietly out of the sheets and onto my knees. I was about to pray for the first time since I was a kid. My prayer was not well-expressed. I hadn't had much practice in sincere prayer, but this time, I spoke to God straight from my heart.

I told Him how Caryl was the good person in our family. She took the kids to church, and she was always pushing me to be a better father and husband. Caryl had continued in her faith even when I didn't support her. I said that I was the bad one who didn't listen—the one who deserved to be sick. I begged Him to help her.

Within a few weeks after this prayer, I went to see the commander of the squadron and asked to be transferred from the helicopter-training pipeline to advanced jet training. My goal was always to be a jet pilot and my grades were good enough and it was worth a try. The transfer came through—which was a miracle in itself—and we were off to Beeville, Texas, where I would fly A-4 Skyhawks.

During our drive west across Interstate 10, Caryl did not have much of an appetite. She was despondent and didn't feel like eating. She just reclined in the front seat with her legs tucked under her and the side of her forehead pressed against the glass window. I was worried. It seemed like she was giving up hope of ever getting better.

Upon arrival in Beeville, Caryl made an appointment to go to the doctor at Fort Sam Houston in San Antonio, where they could administer the injections she needed. When she returned from her first appointment, she was ecstatic.

The doctors said that there was no need for the injections, because her disease was in remission.

I reeled. I couldn't believe what she was telling me. It was too good to be true. How did it happen? What caused the change? I figured it could have been the new, dry climate in Texas or perhaps the fact that she had not eaten much during the move and that fasting had somehow cleansed or reset her system. Now, of course, I know that it was God. He heard my prayer, and now I give Him belated thanks for putting in motion the needed circumstances that allowed Caryl's disease to go into remission.

When I reflect back on this miracle, I am amazed by the sheer mercy of God. I had ignored God up to this point in my life, gladly receiving His blessings and thinking they were the results of my own hard work and determination, not divine grace. When He heard my pathetic prayer that night, God would have been justified in thinking, *Sure,* now *he comes to me.* I cringe when I think about how easy it was for God to see my immaturity—my selfishness. But God didn't care that I was immature and selfish. He just cared that I brought my trouble and my pain to Him.

Why does God care that we come to Him with our troubles? Because my insignificant little prayer demonstrated faith that He exists and is powerful enough to act on our behalf.

Many people may think that God only performs miracles for religious giants like Moses, David, Paul, John, and Peter. Over the years, I have learned that God doesn't perform miracles exclusively for people who are spiritually strong. He often uses miracles to draw weak and wandering souls closer to Him.

. . . .

During a two-and-a-half-hour flight in the A-4 Skyhawk, my instructor complimented me on my procedures and flight skills. He then asked me to make one more approach before we called it a day. I had been flying under a hood—or the bag, as we called it—and could not see anything but my instruments. The instructor gave me directions to turn physical control of the plane over to him when we reached a decision height of eighty-seven feet.

As we approached the end of the runway, I heard the airport tower over my radio headset: "Navy 242, what is your intent?"

"242 request permission to enter the VFR pattern and return to the squadron."

"Roger 242. Turn right to 030 degrees, climb to 1,200 feet and maintain 150 knots. Watch traffic on the right, and enter the landing pattern."

"Roger tower. 242 out."

At that point, I simultaneously rotated the plane to a nose-up position, added full power, turned right to 030 degrees, and began retracting the speed brakes, flaps, and landing gear. I was anticipating that the instructor would take control of the aircraft as he had directed, but he never did. At that moment, I got vertigo and over-rotated the nose of the airplane, placing it in a stall. It took mere seconds for all of this to happen, and I recall realizing that I was too low to eject. I heard the instructor scream. Through a small opening in the bag, I could see his hands clutching the dashboard in front of him.

Just before I passed out, I remember saying, "Oh, God, help me."

"He brought me forth also into a large place;
he delivered me, because he delighted in me."
(Psalm 18:19)

The next thing I remember was hearing the voice from the tower screaming at me through my radio for flying too fast through the landing pattern. Eventually, the instructor took control of the airplane and landed. He got out of the plane and stalked off without saying a word to me, and I never saw him again. The medics pulled me from the plane and took me to the sickbay, where I spent the four days of Thanksgiving weekend crawling on my hands and knees, recovering from the vertigo.

My flight career was over, and no matter how hard I tried, I would not be allowed to fly a military aircraft again. But despite the disappointment, I knew that something very special had happened to me that day. My life had been spared.

. . . .

"When thou art in tribulation, and all these
things are come upon thee, even in the latter

days, if thou turn to the LORD thy God, and shalt
be obedient unto his voice; (For the LORD thy
God is a merciful God;) he will not forsake thee,
neither destroy thee, nor forget the covenant
of thy fathers which he sware unto them"
(Deuteronomy 4:30-31).

After the A-4 Skyhawk incident, I transitioned into the
infantry rather than take my discharge. I didn't want to give
up the challenge of leading Marines. When my tour of active
duty was up, I remained in the reserves for several years.

Once, during summer camp, my unit, Kilo Company
3rd Battalion 25 Marines was out in the Atlantic Ocean,
preparing to come ashore for two weeks of war games. I was
a rifle company commander at the time, and I had received
orders from the battalion commander to report to his ship,
the USS *Okinawa*. He instructed me to wait on the second
deck for a seaman, who would escort me to the helicopter he
had sent for me.

I stood on a little bridge one deck under the flight deck
in front of a little waiting room. I was blankly staring at the
water when I heard a voice say, "Go sit in the corner."

Having heard that message over and over as a child, I
immediately went to the corner of the little waiting room,
sat down on the floor, and pulled my helmet over my face.
Just as I did this, a seaman from the flight deck came diving
through the door, yelling, "Collision!"

The rear rotor blades of the chopper coming to get
me hit the rear rotor blades of a chopper sitting on deck.

Both exploded, killing seven marines and sailors. Burning magnesium came pouring over the side of the deck, covering the spot where I had been standing moments before.

At the time, I marveled at how lucky I was. But there was still that strange voice . . .

. . . .

It was about this time that the awakening began. One not-so-special Sunday morning, I was preparing to go golfing with a few buddies, and Caryl and the kids were preparing to go to Sunday school. My five-year-old son decided to cop an attitude and told his mother, "I don't want to go to church. Why do I have to go?"

"You have to come to church with me," Caryl said sternly.

"If Dad doesn't have to go, then I don't have to either," he said with a scowl.

When Caryl told me what he said, I headed for his room, ready to give him a lecture explaining why he had to go. Before I got to his door, Caryl said in her best do-not-argue-with-me-when-you-know-I'm-right voice, "You need to set the example."

I sighed. I wasn't that good of a golfer, anyway. I got dressed and went with them. They attended the chapel on base, which had a very eclectic congregation of servicemen. The pastor was a Navy chaplain who had served in Vietnam, and I really liked him. The music was terrific. I was surprised when the patriotic hymns gave me goose bumps. Afterward, I stayed and talked to the chaplain, whose soft-spoken yet direct manner impressed me. Before I knew it, I was hooked. We were going to church as a family.

Upon discharge, I moved my family back to Pittsburgh, and we continued to go to church as a family. This time, I made a commitment and was baptized—sprinkled, actually. From that point on, we were churchgoing folk. When we moved to Ohio and California, our first stop was always to find a church that we liked, and then we bought a home nearby. It felt natural.

REVELATION

No man can come to me, except the Father which hath sent me draw him: and I will raise him up at the last day.

—John 6:44

Once I was finished with active duty, my career skyrocketed. I joined a great Midwest, family-run company, and I was rewarded for hard work and discipline. I soon moved my family from Pittsburgh to Ohio so I could take a promotion. There we attended a beautiful little church in the country where we fit in well.

Once during a Sunday school class, an older lady said something to me that I never forgot. While discussing our Scripture lesson, she turned to me and said that I should be the one teaching the class and not the pastor. She didn't say it to disparage the pastor. She said it in a way that was almost surreal, like she was prophesying. The strangest part was that I felt like I *was* supposed to be teaching the class. My brain told me that the idea was irrational. I had never gone to seminary or studied to be a pastor. But I had that feeling nonetheless. "Feeling" isn't the best word to describe it, anyhow. It wasn't a feeling, as in "I feel like eating" or "I feel like watching a movie." It was more of an urge—a tugging. It was something outside of me.

I continued to prosper in my career, and soon it was time to make another move—to Orange County, California. There we struggled with the mind-blowing cost of living, ceaseless traffic snaking through suburbs as far as the eye can see, and frenetically rushed way that southern Californians lived their lives. Everything was bigger in California—including life's problems. It wasn't long before we had joined the rat race.

It was about this time that I began to feel discontented. All the success I experienced at work didn't seem to matter much anymore. Caryl had gone back to school and was working to keep herself occupied, while the kids were busy living their own lives. My life was great, but it was also falling apart. I excelled in my job, but there was no challenge in it. I loved my family, but there was a disconnect between us. I had everything I wanted, but I had no peace. I knew that something had to change.

Caryl and I had both been teaching Sunday school at a nice community church we attended. As I prepared my lessons, I kept finding inequities between the church's doctrine and the Bible. Why didn't we have to be baptized to join the church or participate in feet-washing, and why didn't we anoint the sick? When I finally went to the pastor to discuss what I thought were blatant discrepancies, I felt surely there was something we could do about them.

At the end of my third session, the pastor told me something that seemed crazy: "The only way you are going to be happy is if you leave and find something else. This church is not going to change. Apparently, you have outgrown it."

I was stunned. My personal and professional life were out of whack, and the one thing I had counted on the most for solid footing—the church—had begun to sway back and forth like a child's teeter-totter. I felt like I had just fallen off that teeter-totter, and the playground bully had just punched me in the gut.

I had a million questions. Why wouldn't the church want to do the things that Christ commanded in the Bible? What was so difficult about that? After all, He showed us the way. And why was I so depressed? Most of all, why couldn't I find the answers I was looking for?

I prayed, but God was silent. The soul-searching continued for months, and I continued on a downward spiral. At one of my lowest moments, I found myself sitting on the edge of my bed, complaining to God. "Why is all of this happening?" I asked. "Why isn't there joy in my heart? What is missing from my life?"

That night, I prayed harder than I had ever prayed. I remember saying, "Lord, I will do anything for you. I will go anywhere at any time, no matter what the cost. Please, just help me get it together."

When I finally stopped talking and sat quietly for a moment, I saw in my mind a deep, infinite void. It was like outer space, except someone had scattered the stars, so it was just inky blackness. Then a shaft of light, appearing like a pinpoint far off in the distance, began racing toward me, getting bigger and bigger, coming faster and faster as it grew nearer. When the light entered my thought stream, I heard these words: "You have to love your family."

"I *do* love my family," I responded adamantly.

He said, "No, you must love them as I love the world."

At that moment, I got up and opened our nightstand drawer where I kept a New Testament and some other reading materials. When I was a young boy, I had been given that Bible as a gift for memorizing the names of the books of the Bible in my Sunday school class. I had forgotten that it was there. It fell open to John 14, and the topic was God's love.

. . . .

Beginning that night, God gave me an insatiable appetite for His Word. In just a couple of weeks, my nightly reading had gone from a just few minutes to an hour or more. Caryl and I immediately started to make plans to search for a new church home. We were determined to visit every church in Orange County and find one that obeyed all the commandments of Christ and exhibited the love that the apostle John had written about.

One night shortly after this phenomenon developed, I was traveling on business, and I called home to say hello to Caryl. After we talked for a few minutes, she told me that my cousin, Ken, had phoned and said that he was stopping in California before continuing on to Mexico to do some missionary work. He asked if he could stay at our home. Caryl and I always welcomed visitors, and this was no exception. I had not seen Ken in several years, and it would be nice to catch up.

When I got home from my business trip on Friday evening, Ken had already arrived. He was sitting at the piano, playing hymns, while Caryl was preparing dinner. We greeted one another, and I asked him to continue playing as I sat on the sofa, listening.

Something was dreadfully wrong. As Ken played one song after another, blending the transitions so it all sounded like one long medley, I began to cry. I couldn't control myself. It was a cry that welled up from somewhere deep inside of me. I felt like I was a little boy again, attending church with Grandpap and Gram in Glassport, Pennsylvania.

From time to time, Ken would look over his shoulder, smile at me, and then flow seamlessly into another hymn. He was doing this on purpose! He was playing hymns that were housed deep in my memory—but how did he know? The hymns began to speak to me. "Blessed assurance, Jesus is mine." "Amazing grace, how sweet the sound." "In the garden, He walks with me and talks with me." He played until Caryl called us for dinner. Ken knew why he was there. God had sent him on an errand in addition to the missionary work still ahead of him in Mexico. He came to show me the way.

At the dinner table, we began talking with Ken about his ministry. Ken had grown up in the same church as my grandfather and Caryl's great, great-grandfather, The Church of Jesus Christ that is headquartered in Monongahela, Pennsylvania. He had been baptized when he was thirteen, and much later, had been ordained into the ministry.

As we spoke, I told him about the challenges we were facing at the church we currently attended. I shared with him my disappointments with the hierarchy and the gap between church practice and Christ's commandments. I explained that even after serving with this congregation for several years, we did not feel real, brotherly love. He listened patiently and then told us that there was a branch of his church, The Church of Jesus Christ, in Orange County. He recommended that we visit.

Caryl and I agreed. Ken then told us that the minister of the church lived only a couple of miles from my home. Ken called, and then we went to their home and paid them a visit. Caryl and I liked them instantly and found their hospitality and love captivating. They also invited us to attend a service and we promised them that we would add The Church of Jesus Christ to our list for visitation.

CONVERSION

Caryl and I kept our promise, and as soon as our Sunday school responsibilities were finished, we walked through the doors of The Church of Jesus Christ in Anaheim. Needless to say, it was a very interesting morning. The first thing I noticed was that the building was in need of remodeling. The ministers did not appear to be very well-organized—almost like they hadn't planned anything out ahead of time. There was no choir, just congregational singing. But all the church members—who called one another "brother" and "sister," just as I remember them doing in my youth—seemed to be very close to one another. We could feel it.

After a few hymns and an opening prayer, the preaching began. As soon as the sermon was over, Caryl and I headed for the door. We had made lunch arrangements with a friend, and it was already noon. As we were leaving, two of the ministers followed us to the door to see why we were going so soon. They informed us that they still had the testimony service ahead. We were not aware of their worship practices and explained why we needed to leave. We promised to return for the entire service at some future date.

Before I turned to walk out, I heard myself saying to the two ministers, "I don't think that you know what you have here. There are thousands of people who need to have the love of Jesus Christ in their lives like you have here."

. . . .

A couple of weeks passed, and we did return. We sat toward the front so that we would not miss anything. The preaching was nice, and I heard some things, like the apostasy, the restoration and the Divine commission that I did not understand, so my interest was piqued. It felt good.

The minister then announced that the service was open for anyone who wanted to stand and publicly share a testimony. The purpose of the testimony service was to honor and glorify God for what He had done for us personally—especially our salvation. People stood up and thanked God for specific things, like helping them through a difficult situation at work, or broad things like salvation and grace. *What a* neat *thing to do during church,* I thought.

An elderly woman to my left stood by, pulling herself up while holding onto the pew in front of her. I don't think that she was more than five feet tall. She looked straight at me and began to weep. I had never met this woman before, and I could not imagine why she was behaving this way. When she spoke, she pointed her finger at me and spoke in broken English with a heavy Italian accent. "This man is a-no stranger. His grandapap bapatized me in 1938 in Greensburg, Pennsylvania. When I saw his-a face, I knew him from before."

I began crying. My heart, or maybe my spirit, was trembling within me, but at the same time, I did not fully understand what was happening. This woman, who I later learned was called Sister Nancy, finally sat down, but I could hear many members of the congregation crying quietly in their seats. I tried to contain myself, but little did I know that things were just beginning.

To Sister Nancy's left sat another elderly woman whose name was Sister Mary. As she rose to her feet, I saw that she had a crumpled handkerchief in her hand, and she, too, was looking at me. She said quietly and humbly, "As most of you know, I lived in Glassport, Pennsylvania for many years before moving here to California with my daughter. And I lived across the street from this man's grandfather and grandmother. In the early years of my marriage, my husband treated me very badly. Many of you know that he was unfaithful—and often times brutal with me. This man's grandmother would take me in and bind my wounds. One day, his grandfather talked with my husband about being a good spouse. From that day forward, my husband never hurt me again."

By this point, I was a basket case. All I wanted was for the meeting to be over so that we could escape. I had no idea a church service could be so emotional. I did not like feeling that my emotions were not within my control, but at the same time, I felt something wonderful—something I had not felt for a long time. I felt stillness—a peace that told me I had found my way home and that my family was there, waiting for me to return. I didn't know it at the time, but I was experiencing an outpouring of love from people whom I barely knew. Could this be what Jesus meant when he said,

> "A new commandment I give unto you, That ye love one another; as I have loved you, that ye also love one another. By this shall all men know that ye are my disciples, if ye have love one to another" (John 13:34-35).

. . . .

After a few more visits to The Church of Jesus Christ, I began to think rationally. Although I had felt an extraordinary love from the members of this church, there were a few technical things that irked me. For example, I did not like the fact that I could not participate in communion. This church has a rule stating that you have to be a baptized member of their church to take communion during their services. I had already been baptized in another church, but they insisted that I had to be baptized in *their* church—under their doctrine and under the hands of their ministry—to share the Lord's Supper with them. I was also very uncomfortable with the fact that they practiced feet-washing once a quarter.

I laid all my questions out to the ministry. They patiently explained that everything they practiced was directed by Christ, and they showed me the Scriptures to prove it. But no matter how logically presented the ideas were, they were not sinking in. Somehow, I was backtracking on everything that had once made me so dissatisfied with my previous church. There I had argued with the pastor, saying we needed to be true to the Scriptures, and now I was trying to escape that same truth, because I did not want to be held accountable to it.

I was determined to start visiting other churches, as I had planned. Riding home one afternoon, I told Caryl of my decision to resume visiting other churches. She asked, "Why? Why don't you want to stay here? Isn't this what we said was missing?"

I looked over to her side of the car, but she had craned her neck toward the window. In the reflection, I could see tears rolling down her cheeks. Obviously she felt passionately about the church, but I was determined to shop around.

We agreed to make one final visit to The Church of Jesus Christ. That Sunday, I made sure we sat near the rear of the church so that I could escape quickly when the service was over. When the ministers walked onto the rostrum, there was another man with them—a visiting minister from another branch of the church. He was an older Italian man whom they later introduced as Apostle Joseph Lovalvo. I took one look at him and whispered sideways to Caryl, "We need to leave."

She looked at me, annoyed, since she was trying to sing the opening hymn, and asked, "Why?"

"When I was little and Grandpap took me to church, the old Italian ministers would stand up, take off their jackets, roll up their sleeves, produce a large handkerchief out of their back pockets, and lay it on the pulpit. Then, they would start speaking in English with their heavy accents, but when they got really worked up, they would start to cry and use the handkerchief. With the hanky in front of their mouth and the broken English, it was impossible to understand them. When this guy gets going, we won't understand a thing."

Caryl threatened me with physical harm if I spoke again.

Sure enough, when the presiding minister introduced Brother Joe and Brother Joe mounted the rostrum, the first thing he did was take off his jacket and roll up his sleeves.

Then, out came the oversized hanky. I readied myself for the worst, but to my surprise, I got to hear the best.

Brother Joe started speaking, and for the next forty-five minutes, I was riveted to my seat. He started preaching about each of the concerns that I had been struggling with. In detail, he thoroughly answered my every question. *How could he have known?* I thought. I didn't even discuss some of my concerns with Caryl, yet one by one, as if checking them off a list, he spoke until each issue was crystal clear—and never once in broken English.

The drive home was longer than usual. Neither Caryl nor I spoke much.

. . . .

That same night, I had to go to San Diego to attend a sales meeting for work starting first thing Monday morning. When I arrived in San Diego, I remembered that I was supposed to go to dinner with my boss and other coworkers, but I just didn't have the heart. Instead, I found myself pacing around my room, trying to digest all that had happened in the last six weeks since my cousin Ken's visit. My boss, Allan, called me and told me I was going to be late if I did not get down to the lobby, but I begged off and told him I would see him at breakfast.

After a restless night, I dragged myself out of bed and got dressed to go to breakfast, but the questions on my mind were so pressing that I stayed in my room and just paced back and forth, all the while talking out loud to God and sharing with him all my conflict, frustrations, and hesitations.

Finally, after two days of fasting and prayer—although I did not realize what I was doing—I called Caryl and told her that I had decided to become a member of The Church of Jesus Christ. I would submit myself to rebaptism and whatever else I had to do. Her response surprised me. "It is about time. I have been waiting four weeks for you."

Caryl had already made up her mind, but she did not want to put any pressure on me to do the same. She knew I had to make my own decision. Once again, she had taken spiritual leadership while I was still arm wrestling with God.

. . . .

> Bring ye all the tithes into the storehouse, that there may be meat in mine house, and prove me now herewith, saith the LORD of hosts, if I will not open you the windows of heaven, and pour you out a blessing, that there shall not be room enough to receive it. (Malachi 3:10)

Caryl and I met with the two ministers, Brothers Walt and Jim that week, and they questioned us to determine if we understood what we were doing. We each explained why we wanted to be baptized in The Church of Jesus Christ, and we expressed our love for the brothers and sisters of the church, who had loved us first. We told them that it felt like we were coming home. As Sister Nancy had said, "He is a-no stranger."

After we prayed together, we agreed to be baptized the following Sunday. The brothers left, and Caryl and I felt like we were floating. Our spirits were light, and we were filled with joy. Nothing external had changed in our lives.

We still had the same jobs, lived in the same home, and had the same relationship with our kids, but we could feel that something good was about to happen. We knew that we had made a decision that would bless the rest of our lives.

We were at church early Sunday morning, dressed in our white baptismal suits. Caryl and I were sitting together, waiting for the others to arrive so we could all carpool to the Colorado Lagoon, the site where the church normally holds baptisms. She looked at me and asked, "Why are you crying?" I felt like I did when Ken was playing those old hymns at our home. I was not in control. I felt like my insides were quaking, and I had no power to quiet them. Then Caryl said, "Last night as I was praying, I asked God which minister would bring me back into the Lord's presence. After I waited, I heard a voice, and it said that Brother Otto would bring me back into God's presence."

This confused her, because the minister who was going to baptize her was Brother Jim. She also said that she felt like she was shaking inside, although you couldn't see it on the outside.

At the Colorado Lagoon, the first thing that the congregation did was offer prayer and sing a hymn. Then the two brothers asked us each two questions: "Have you repented of all of your sins, and do you promise to serve God all the days of your life?"

Caryl and I both said, "Yes!" Caryl, the two ministers, and I walked into the waist-deep water. Caryl was a little more nervous than me, because she had always been afraid of water. I was only a few feet away and encouraged her not to be afraid.

I watched as the minister, Brother Jim, raised his right hand and said in a loud voice, "Caryl DiBattista, having authority given me of Jesus Christ, I baptize you in the name of the Father, the Son, and the Holy Ghost. Amen." Then he immediately immersed her in the water. When she emerged, I could not believe my eyes. Caryl is a beautiful woman, but when I saw her face, wet and shining, it was indescribably beautiful. She was glowing from within. It was like she was about to explode with life—new life. She had indeed been *born again*.

Next, Brother Walt did exactly the same thing as Brother Jim had done—only this time, it was for me. As I went under the water, it seemed like I was there for a while, and as I emerged, I immediately noticed that I felt lighter. An apparent load had been taken off of my shoulders. A burden that I hadn't even recognized that I carried had been lifted. My sins were gone. I, too, had been born again *of the water*.

> "Jesus answered, Verily, verily, I say unto thee,
> Except a man be born of water and of the Spirit,
> he cannot enter into the kingdom of God."
> (John 3:5)

I looked at Caryl, and she said, "John, I feel like I could dance on the water!"

We turned to the shore, and what I saw was unreal. The sky had never been so blue, even in California. The trees were an incredible bright green, and the water was crystal clear. The twenty or thirty people on the shore were the most beautiful people that I had ever seen in my life. They were all smiling at us, and some had tears rolling down their cheeks. The sun was shining upon them, causing a golden aura to appear around the group. As deaconesses, Sisters Nancy and Mary were there to greet Caryl and drape a towel around her as she exited the water. We sang the old hymn, "A New Name Written Down in Glory." Then the people in the crowd enveloped Caryl and me with hugs and kisses.

> "John answered, saying unto them all, I indeed baptize you with water; but one mightier than I cometh, the latchet of whose shoes I am not worthy to unloose: he shall baptize you with the Holy Ghost and with fire." (Luke 3:16)

Back at the church, Caryl and I changed our clothes and prepared to have prayer offered by the ministry so that we would receive the gift of the Holy Ghost. Everything was done in the perfect order as written in the Scriptures and demonstrated by Christ and His apostles. Caryl was to be prayed for first, and she told me that she was still shaking inside. I was, too.

All of the ministry knelt and offered prayer, asking God to bless them as they were about to perform the holy ordinance. When they stood, Brother Otto stepped forward, laid his hands on Caryl's head, and started to pray. As he was coming to the end of his prayer, his right hand went into the air, and he confirmed the gift of the Holy Ghost upon her in a voice that was filled with power.

Caryl came back to the pew and said that the shaking had stopped. She felt something very wonderful when Otto finished his prayer. She explained that her body felt as if she was filled with warm oil, and a peaceful calmness fell on her unlike anything she had ever experienced before.

As I went to the chair, Brother Otto began to tell the congregation, "While praying for our new sister, Caryl, my right hand went up in the air, and I felt fire enter it and flow through my hands as they were upon her head."

Truly, Caryl had been baptized *by the Holy Ghost and with fire.*

> But the manifestation of the Spirit is given to every man to profit withal. For to one is given by the Spirit the word of wisdom; to another the word of knowledge by the same Spirit; To another faith by the same Spirit; to another the gifts of healing by the same Spirit; To another the working of miracles; to another prophecy; to another discerning of spirits; to another divers kinds of tongues; to another the interpretation of tongues: But all these worketh that one and the selfsame Spirit, dividing to every man severally as he will. (1 Corinthians 12:7-11)

The reception of the Holy Ghost was not as dramatic for me. The shaking stopped, but there were no other manifestations of God's Spirit, and as I walked back to the pew, I confess that I felt like I had made a mistake.

I shouldn't have done this, I said to myself. I wasn't ready to make this commitment. I didn't take it seriously enough. I did not pray enough. This time another spirit was influencing my thoughts, but it wasn't from God.

The service was almost over when Caryl stood up and asked the entire congregation to come to our home for dinner that night. I couldn't believe it. The last thing that I wanted was to see all the people again that evening while feeling the way that I did.

．．．．

At home, Caryl was in the kitchen, making dinner, joyfully singing while I was up in our bedroom on my knees, having a sincere talk with God. I wanted Him to tell me whether or not I did the right thing. Caryl would holler, "Hey, I need some help down here," and I would reluctantly go and assist her for a few minutes and then disappear into the bedroom again for more discussion with God. I admitted that I had not taken my baptism seriously enough. I confessed all my sins again, and I asked for a manifestation—a revelation, a confirmation—to show me that I had done the right thing. But I got nothing, and Caryl was still singing downstairs.

Finally, Satan had me so confused, I was convinced that I was not worthy enough to be baptized or receive God's grace. I sat in a chair and stared down the steps at the front door in a stupor of shame and guilt, thinking that I had just made the biggest mistake of my life.

Just then, the doorbell rang, and Caryl rushed to our double doors and flung them both wide. There stood about twenty of the brothers and sisters from the church. One of our ministers, Brother Jim; his wife, Sister Lynette; and their two kids were in front of the group. These were the people Ken had taken Caryl and me to meet when he was at my home.

I looked at their big smiles, and I saw something moving from them toward me. There seemed to be a distortion in the air—almost like a cloud, but it was clear and floating up the steps toward me. As I watched this phenomena approach and engulf me, I felt a love so great that I began to weep. Caryl, knowing that there was something wrong, sent Jim up to see me immediately. He found me weeping and sobbing.

I explained what happened, and he interpreted the event. He said, "John, Satan is trying to unsettle you by filling your mind with doubt about the choice you made today. When your doors opened, you saw something. It was the love of the saints. God allowed you to actually see it so you would understand something. He wants you to understand that while it's great to see the manifestations of God's power, it is not the most important thing. The most important thing is obeying His commandments and loving God more than anything else. That is what you did today when you were baptized. This is the key to the gospel of Jesus Christ—obedience and love!"

Over time, I have come to fully understand the truth of those words. If we cannot love God and each other, we become like the person Paul described in 1 Corinthians 13:1:

"Though I speak with the tongues of men and of angels, and have not charity (love), I am become as sounding brass, or a tinkling cymbal."

Love is the central theme of the gospel. Jesus taught His disciples repeatedly to love God and to love one another. In fact, His teachings were not new. They were the same commandments that Moses taught the children of Israel when they came out of Egypt.

"God is love; and he that dwelleth in love dwelleth in God, and God in him" (1 John 4:16).

How simple, yet difficult, it is to love God and our neighbors. It's tricky to set aside everything the world has told us to love—power, prestige, wealth, beauty, self-truths—and replace it with a love for God first and for others before ourselves.

MILK

After our baptisms, Caryl and I began attending every meeting and function that was offered at church, and I began studying the Scriptures fervently.

The Church of Jesus Christ is a restoration church, and its history is more complex than most. This church is often confused with the Mormon (or Latter-Day Saints) church, because it shares a similar name and recognizes the Book of Mormon as the holy word of God. But we are not affiliated with the Mormon Church, and our beliefs are actually quite different.

The Church of Jesus Christ was restored and legally formed in 1830 by Joseph Smith, Oliver Cowdery, and Martin Harris after they had read the Book of Mormon, which was translated from a set of ancient gold plates—the discovery of which is a story in itself! Soon after the church's inception, the church leadership allowed many false revelations to enter into the faith. They began practicing things that could not be supported by Scripture, such as plurality of gods, plurality of wives, the Aaronic priesthood, degrees of glory, and more.

In 1844, Joseph Smith, who was the leader of the church, and his brother were murdered in Carthage, Illinois. This led to a struggle for leadership of the church, which boasted more than 210,000 converts. Most church members followed Brigham Young to Utah and became known as Mormons, or the Church of Jesus Christ of Latter-Day Saints. The second largest group of members became the Reorganized Church of Jesus Christ, headquartered in Independence, Missouri. The original Church of Jesus Christ—the church I had just joined—was led to Pennsylvania by the first counselor to the president, Sidney Rigdon. A few years later, a convert of Rigdon's—a man named William Bickerton—legally established it in 1862 as The Church of Jesus Christ, headquartered in Green Oak, Pennsylvania.

This brief sketch does not do the history justice, but it suffices to communicate that I had a great deal of research and study to do in order to satisfy myself that I had found the truth. People have spent lifetimes trying to digest the Bible, let alone another record. I had my work cut out for me.

I began studying and reading the Bible and the Book of Mormon voraciously in an attempt to get caught up. I realized that I needed a mentor and teacher. I did not know whom to go to, and there was no formal program outside of our regular new members' classes. So I reached out to God. I had read that fasting and praying was the method used by others to get responses from the Lord, so I decided to try it. I embarked on a three-day fast.

During the third day, I was working with a representative of my company in Livermore, California, and the Spirit spoke to me and told me to go to Brother Joseph Lovalvo's home in Modesto, California. Brother Joe would help me. Modesto wasn't very far from Livermore, so the trip was completely doable. But I hesitated, because I didn't know Brother Joe very well. I had only had seen him one time in Anaheim when he preached the sermon that answered all my questions. He was one of the twelve apostles, and on top of that, he was the president of the

Quorum of Twelve, which basically meant that he was the spiritual leader of the church. I didn't think that he would have time for me.

The Spirit spoke again. "Go see Brother Joe."

I gave in and drove one hour to Modesto. I found Brother Joe's house, but no one answered the door. I went to a public phone and looked up the phone number of his son, Leonard. Leonard told me that his mom had just had knee surgery and that his dad, Brother Joe, was at the hospital sitting with her.

Armed with the directions Brother Leonard gave me, I headed to the hospital only to find the information desk closed. How was I going to find Brother Joe in a hospital of this size? What I thought would be a simple visit had turned into a song and dance. Surely obeying God wasn't this difficult. I bowed my head and offered prayer. "Lord, I came here because you commanded me to. Please help me find Brother Joe."

When I finished, I looked down one of the long corridors that began at the lobby, and standing at an intersection directly under a fluorescent light was Brother Joe. After picking up my jaw from the floor, I walked over to him and introduced myself. After visiting his wife, Sister Virginia, we went to a nearby restaurant and had a bowl of soup.

Brother Joe asked why I had come, and I told him simply, "God sent me. I need someone to teach me the history of the church." I could see tears in his eyes as he immediately began to explain the restoration story to me.

That night, we sat in his living room until 2:00 a.m. discussing Scripture. Then he laid his hands on my head and prayed, asking God to help me understand the complete gospel of Christ. Looking back, I recognize that this was a very special moment in my life.

. . . .

Brother Joe took our mentoring relationship seriously. My instructions were to come to his home in Modesto once a month for an entire weekend so he could teach me the Scriptures. So it began. Caryl and I would make the six-hour drive every month to his home. We would arrive Friday night in time for a little conversation and a snack before bed. Beginning Saturday morning after breakfast, we would sit at the kitchen table for hours at a time, studying, listening, asking questions, and taking notes.

The blessings during these precious times were incredible. Brother Joe had experienced many wonderful things in his ministry. He was truly a man of God. We seemed to spend most of the time crying as we listened to his stories of healing the sick, raising the dead, and souls coming to Christ. He knew—but I didn't—that he was setting the bar for my future ministry.

During those sessions, Caryl and I witnessed one of the most beautiful expressions of love that we had ever seen in our lives. As Joe was teaching, he would suddenly stop and look at his wife of more than fifty years and say, "Virgi," (short for Virginia) "I love you, honey." He would then reach over and kiss her.

Not only did Brother Joe teach the gospel of love, but he also demonstrated it to his family, friends, and all people he came in contact with. He showed me that one cannot propagate the gospel to strangers without first showing it to those closest to himself. The demonstration of God's love must start with our families.

One year later, at the end of our Saturday session, Brother Joe said something that was very difficult for me to believe. "John, I have taught you all that you need to know. It's time to ask God what he wants you to do in the church."

I resisted. I didn't want these days to end. But Brother Joe continued, "Tonight, we are going to pray and ask God to send an angel to tell you what he wants you to do in the church."

Whoa, I thought. *What faith!* I had never heard anyone so bold. He spoke like he and God were friends.

We both knelt down in the living room, and he began to pray out loud. And just as he had said, he asked God to send an angel to me that night. I don't know why, but I opened my eyes and turned my head to look at his face. It was lifted up toward heaven, and it was radiating light. I remember hoping that he wouldn't ask me to pray, because I knew that I could not pray like that.

· · · ·

I joined Caryl in the small guest room and quickly fell asleep. At 5:00 a.m., I awoke and looked at the clock. I rolled over to return to sleep when someone began shaking my left shoulder. I knew that Caryl was to my right, and there was only a nightstand on my left-hand side. I closed my eyes tight and ignored what I was feeling. Again, someone shook me as if to say, "Get up!" And again, I closed my eyes even tighter, not wanting to look over my shoulder, because in my mind, I knew no one could be there. The third time, my spirit was shaken loose from my body and began ascending upward. I saw my body and Caryl lying in the bed below. I passed through the ceiling without any sensation and found myself standing in front of a personage.

A Book of Mormon prophet wrote in 1 Nephi 11:11, "And I said unto him: To know the interpretation thereof—for I spake unto him as a man speaketh; for I beheld that he was in the form of a man; yet nevertheless, I knew that it was the Spirit of the Lord; and he spake unto me as a man speaketh with another."

This describes what I experienced. I stood before this personage, and He told me what I should do. I argued that what He asked of me was impossible, given my sinful background. As proof, I began to confess all the bad things that I had done in my life. As I did this, He just kept shaking his head up and down like He knew all of this already. Then it dawned on me—He *did* know. Of course He did. He died for all of those sins and made me a new man the day I was baptized. Nevertheless, I urged Him to get someone else for this job—someone better than me, someone who had been born and raised in the church and was more righteous than me. But He just kept gently speaking to me until I submitted and took His direction.

When He was finished, I turned to walk away. As I did, He called me by name: "John."

I can't begin to describe to you the feeling that I had when the living God of heaven and earth—the resurrected Christ—calls you by your first name. Filled with humility and awe, I turned and asked, "Yes, Master?"

He said, "There is one more thing that you must do."

"Yes, Lord, what is it?" I quietly asked.

"You must *tell them how much I love them*," He said.

As I stared at this personage, it started to take the form of a human body. The hair, eyes, and white robe came into focus. It was my Lord and Savior. It was Jesus Christ.

I wanted to fall on the ground and begin to worship Him, hold His feet, and weep tears of joy. I didn't want to leave His presence, but just as these things entered my mind, I reentered my body. I noticed that it was 5:21 a.m. I was with Him for twenty-one minutes. I immediately went back to sleep and slept until the alarm went off at 8:00. I was so overcome by what I had experienced that I did not talk much in the morning. In fact, I was not sure if I had dreamed this, imagined it, or if it had really happened.

The four of us had breakfast, got ready for church, and left for Sunday school. There were only a handful of people there, but I enjoyed the class. Afterward, we had a short break before the morning preaching service started. Brother Leonard was the minister in charge, and he asked if I would like to sit on the rostrum. I declined. I held no formal church office, and I was still unsure of what had happened to me that night.

Just as the morning service was about to begin and the members of the congregation were settling into their seats, Brother Paul, who was then the first counselor to the president of the church, entered the building. He lived in Pittsburgh, Pennsylvania but was working that week in San Francisco, so he made the short drive to Modesto for the service.

I whispered to Caryl excitedly, "We are going to have a great meeting today."

Brother Paul and Brother Joe were both apostles and were both excellent speakers. Just then, Brother Joe came off the rostrum and walked to where Caryl and I were sitting. He smiled broadly and said, "I want you to sit up front today." He then added, "Just to get the feel for it."

He had to pry my hands off the pew's armrest, but I eventually got up and followed him to the pulpit. I found myself staring out over the congregation, wondering what would happen next.

The service opened with spirit-filled singing and prayer. Brother Paul stepped to the pulpit and began preaching a beautiful message about various characters from the New Testament—the woman who suffered from a blood disease for twelve years; Zaccheus, the short-statured tax collector; and Bartimaeus, the blind man who sat by the road. He explained how all three had to do something extra to get

Jesus' attention and receive their healing. The woman had to press through a crowd to touch the hem of Jesus' garment. Zaccheus had to climb a tree to see above the crowd. Bartimaeus had to cry with a loud voice, even after many told him to be quiet.

Brother Paul then asked, "What are *you* willing to do to get Jesus' attention?"

The Spirit was blessing the congregation as he spoke, and you could see that people were deeply contemplating his words.

When he finished, Brother Leonard asked me to stand and give my testimony. By this time, I was gripping my chair with both hands. I had started feeling a strange sensation as Brother Paul was finishing his sermon. I felt an energy emanating from my entire body, especially from my head. Quickly, I thought rationally and asked myself, *How hard could this be? You are a salesman, after all, and you have experience speaking in front of large crowds. This is no big deal.*

I walked over to the pulpit and placed both hands on the sides of it. When I did that, my spirit separated from my body again, just as it had the night before. I saw my body beginning to preach, but my spirit was standing two feet behind my body. God was using my body to deliver a message to the congregation, and I was allowed to watch everything in slow motion from the vantage point of my spirit. I looked around and saw that tears were running down the faces of many in the congregation. As my body was being used to deliver this message, concepts and thoughts were coming out of my mouth that only God could have placed there. I listened to myself like I had listened to Grandpap on that bench when I was fourteen years old.

The message was simple yet powerful: the time to build the kingdom of God upon the earth has come. We need to be agents of God to answer Jesus' prayer when He said to the Father, "Thy kingdom come. Thy will be done in earth, as it is in heaven."

This message was not new. All of the ancient prophets had written about it. Many people throughout history dreamed of establishing the kingdom of God on earth and put forth effort to do so. The ancients like Enoch, Noah, Abraham, Melchizedek, David, and Solomon, to name just a few, all desired a better country—that is, a heavenly country the author of Hebrews writes about. The disciples also asked Christ before His ascension if He would restore the kingdom to Israel, but He responded that it was not for them to know. Those who came to America, especially the Puritans and Pilgrims, had in their constitutions the same idea: to build the kingdom of God upon the earth. But it was not to be done in their time.

I continued to explain that in order for God's kingdom to reign on earth, it first has to reign in our hearts. We need to love God more than anything else in our life. He has to come first in all things. It is necessary for us to recognize that no matter what fate brings us, our destiny, as followers of Christ, is to demonstrate to all people the same unconditional love that Christ has for us. These concepts were not new and have been preached from pulpits for centuries. I acknowledged that there is often a gap between what we believe to be true and what we actually do and that it was time to close that gap and demonstrate to the rest of the world that there exists a people with a love so great that any obstacle can be overcome. I said we should show that miracles have not ceased, and the wondrous signs of the Holy Spirit still follow those who correctly believe. I continued by saying that Jesus is alive, and He sits at the right hand of the Father to intercede and help us in building His kingdom.

> "Jesus answered and said unto him, If a man love me, he will keep my words: and my Father will love him, and we will come unto him, and make our abode with him" (John 14:23).

I shared my own personal search to find my life's purpose. We must each travel our own path in order to find our reason for *being*. As we get older, we begin to ask ourselves, *Why was I born? What is the meaning of my life? What are my responsibilities? What does God want me to do, and how does He want me to do it? When I die, what will I have contributed? What will God say when I get to the grave? Will He say, "You have arrived at your death safely"? Or will He say, "Well done, my good and faithful servant"?*

The message rushed over the congregation like a flood. When I finished and sat, everybody remained motionless in pin-drop silence. Brother Joe leaned over to me, and I expected him to make some sort of comment about the message I had just given. Instead, he said something I didn't expect: "John, if you do what the Lord commands you to do, your life will be good. If you don't, your life will be miserable."

Great comfort, I thought. I didn't even understand what had just happened.

Over the next several months, I visited many different branches of the church. If I was asked to speak, I delivered the same message that the Lord gave me that early morning in November. God would never fail to show His power by sending signs and wonders. In other words, people would see visions, the gift of tongues would be spoken, or God would show us something powerful to verify the truth of the message.

As I continued to do what I had been told by God, I began to witness to people everywhere. On airplanes, in meetings at work, or in hotels while on business trips, I always felt the Lord prompting me to share the message with someone. Often, miracles would happen: healings, revelations, and other inexplicable manifestations of his Spirit, just as Jesus promised when he was here on the earth.

"And these signs shall follow them that believe; In my name shall they cast out devils; they shall speak with new tongues; They shall take up serpents; and if they drink any deadly thing, it shall not hurt them; they shall lay hands on the sick, and they shall recover" (Mark 16:7-18).

PURPOSE

And as Jesus passed forth from thence, he saw a man, named Matthew, sitting at the receipt of custom: and he saith unto him, Follow me. And he arose, and followed him.

—Matthew 9:9

The calling into a position of spiritual labor has to be just that—a calling. God decides when He wants to use a person, and then He calls that person, just as He did in the New Testament. Church leadership positions were never intended to be vocations. People don't have the right to take an office upon themselves. God's gifts and power are not ours to command; they are gifts from God to be used to further His kingdom—on His terms.

It was about this time that God showed me I was being called into the ministry. He revealed this to me personally, and He also revealed it to several other people so that my calling could be confirmed by others. The ministry reviewed these revelations, prayed about them, and decided it was time to ordain me as a teacher. Once ordained, I was welcome to preach and teach throughout the church, and I felt a new level of liberty in my spiritual service.

As I grew into my positions of spiritual leadership, I tried my best to rely on God's Spirit to tell me what to do. I wanted to rely on Him for everything—not just big decisions, but also small ones. I tried to listen to Him all the time, but I am not perfect, and there were times when I did not listen. The beauty of Jesus, though, is that He has the power to transform our mistakes into something good. If we learn from our misdeeds, we become stronger Christians. The ugliness of our sins is miraculously reshaped and fashioned into something beautiful when God gets a hold of them. The times when my spiritual maturity grew the most were during periods of great confusion, temptation, and disillusionment.

There was one particular incident in which I failed God. I didn't do what He asked me to do. Although it was a small thing, it had an enormous impact on the way I viewed my life.

I was returning a rental car at the Phoenix airport. I wrote the mileage and the fuel level on the information card and began to exit the car. As I swung my legs out of the car, I had a vision. I saw Peter and John at the gate Beautiful, looking at the crippled man who was begging for alms, an account that can be found in the third chapter of Acts. Peter said to the blind man,

> "Silver and gold have I none; but such as I have give I thee: In the name of Jesus Christ of Nazareth rise up and walk" (Acts 3:6).

When the vision ended, I remained where I was, halfway in and halfway out of the vehicle, pondering what it meant. Then I saw the same vision a second time. When it ended, I exited the car and walked over to the rental car attendant's booth. As I slipped my information card through the slit in the plastic window, I saw that the attendant had two partial arms. They extended to where the elbow should have been.

He had one finger on one stump and two fingers on the other. As I handed him the card, the Spirit of God fell on us both. I knew that all I had to do was say to this young man, "In the name of Jesus Christ of Nazareth, be whole."

But I couldn't do it. There were too many people around, and I was unsure—afraid. What would happen if it did not work? I couldn't find enough faith, not even the size of a grain of mustard seed, to utter those few words. But all the while, my eyes remained locked on this young attendant.

After a few moments, the Spirit passed, and I began walking away. After I had gone a few paces, I heard the attendant call my name, and I returned to see what he wanted. There we stood, face to face again. He looked into my eyes and said, "Mr. DiBattista, I just wanted to say one thing. May God bless you."

My eyes immediately filled with tears, and my heart burned with shame. I realized that I had just broken my promise. I had promised God that I would go anywhere and do anything for Him, no matter the cost. But when the rubber hit the road, I failed.

I hurried to my gate, rushing down the terminal like a man pursued. I sat in the gate waiting area, hunched over like someone who had a piano hanging over His head. I wondered what God would do to me for breaking my promise.

As I sat there, torturing myself, I was surprised to hear someone calling my name. It was Brother Frank, another minister from the church. Coincidently, he and I were on the same flight. Frank saw that I was troubled, and he asked what had happened. After relaying the story to him, I waited for the admonishment that I knew I deserved for what I had done. I braced myself for the worst. But instead of judging me, Frank chuckled. He encouraged me and said that God was teaching me a lesson. It was then that I realized I had not truly exhaled since my encounter with the attendant. I let out a long, haggard breath and closed my eyes. I accepted the mercy that had been extended to me—not because I deserved it, but because Christ died so I could have it.

. . . .

I continued to pray and ask God for forgiveness for my failure with the rental car attendant. It did not take long for Him to give me another opportunity. Phil, a friend and colleague whom I had witnessed to, called me on the phone and asked me to come to the hospital and pray for his mother-in-law, Eleanor, who had just been diagnosed with colon cancer.

When I arrived at the hospital, I found Eleanor filled with fear and clenching the rails on her bed. I tried to calm her by talking about Jesus. I rehearsed the many miracles he performed, and soon the spirit of peace entered the room. She let go of the bed rails and was softly talking to me. The family asked me to offer a prayer, so I knelt by the bed and bowed my head. I heard myself saying, "Lord, when the doctor returns, have him bring a *good report*. Let him say that there has been a mistake, and Eleanor is clear of cancer."

When I finished praying, I said goodbye to Eleanor and her family and walked to my car. Just as I unlocked my door,

I realized that Phil had followed me. When he caught up to me, he began yelling.

"It was a mistake to call you," he spat bitterly. "You gave her false hope! What am I going to tell her when the doctor says that she still has cancer? Why would you do that?"

"I'm sorry you feel that way," I said to Phil. Then I got in the car and left. It was in the Lord's hands.

The following Sunday at church, I was seated in the congregation, waiting for the service to begin, when I felt someone sit down next to me. I was astonished to see that it was Phil. I nodded politely, and he nodded back.

This may get ugly, I thought to myself. *He is probably here to blast me in front of the ministry and the congregation.* But Phil just sat silently and listened to the preaching. When the meeting was opened for testimony, Phil was first on his feet. I slouched down in the pew. Phil's eyes scanned the congregation, and then he pointed at me and related what had happened at the hospital, including the part when he screamed at me in the parking lot. The congregation sat silently, and I could tell that they weren't sure where Phil was going with this.

Then he said, "I owe John an apology. When I returned to Eleanor's room, the doctor walked in behind me. As I was thinking of how I could apologize to my family for asking John to come and pray, the doctor said, 'I've brought a *good report*. There has been a mistake, and Eleanor is clear of cancer.' The doctor had said the exact words that John had used just minutes before in his prayer."

Then Phil went on to thank Jesus Christ for Eleanor's healing. I sat up in the pew, realizing what God had done and the lesson that I had learned. I was determined from that point to try my best to move with the Spirit and never deny Him again. I was going to ignore the comments of people around me and do whatever God requested of me. His opinion is the only one that matters.

. . . .

The ministry in the Anaheim branch where I held my membership felt that I was being called into the priesthood. Once ordained I would have complete authority to perform all the ordinances of the church, including baptizing converts, serving the Lord's Supper, laying hands on the sick, and conducting meetings. The Anaheim ministry took the proposal to the region conference, and a ministerial board was convened.

I felt good as the board questioned my knowledge of the Scriptures as well as the faith and doctrine of the church. The brother who was asking the questions was an apostle, and his knowledge of the church, including its history, was unsurpassed. He challenged me in many areas. Towards the end, the questions became more and more intense, and all of a sudden, an evangelist who was sitting near me spoke in the Spirit, saying, "Thus sayeth the Lord! I have called this one into my ministry."

The board dismissed me for a moment and took the vote. It was decided. I was to be ordained a minister. God had spoken on my behalf.

My ordination date was set for the first Sunday in March, 1991. That morning, the church building was filled beyond capacity, and I was moved by the show of support by the membership and ministry—some who had traveled great distances to attend. Even Brother Joe had driven down from Modesto, and as the senior member of the ministry, he conducted the service.

Brother Joe preached a sermon on the responsibilities of a minister, and I was set apart by the washing of feet. A Guatemalan brother was inspired to perform this ordinance, and as he washed my feet, he prayed in English when he washed the first foot and in Spanish when he washed my other foot. I thought this was unusual, but the Spirit was very strong.

One young man who was visiting the church for the first time with my daughter Chris saw me holding a rotating globe in my hands. Not knowing why I would do this, he leaned over to Chris and asked, "Why is your dad holding a globe?"

"A what?" she whispered.

"A globe, like a mini version of the world. Is there some special significance behind this?"

"My dad," she said, "my dad isn't holding a globe. He isn't holding anything."

After the meeting ended, Chris brought her friend to me. They asked me what was going on, and I understood immediately that this young man had seen a vision, and the interpretation of the vision was that my ministry was one day going to include worldwide travel.

About the time that this young man was having the vision during the service, the ministers were proceeding with the actual ordination. The ministers first knelt together in prayer, asking God to direct the proceedings. After they rose, they waited until the Spirit of God directed one minister to anoint me with blessed oil and offer the prayer that would ordain me into the ministry. It seemed like a long time until Brother Joe extended his hand and took the oil. It was a great privilege for my mentor to ordain me into the priesthood of the Son of God.

There were several beautiful confirmations that day, but none as wonderful as the Word of the Lord that came to a Mexican sister. He said through her, "Walk without fear, for I will be with you—always by your side to help you when you need me—because I chose you to be a light on the earth and to preach my Word wherever you may be."

I have cherished these words and relied on them many times, especially while traveling in countries around the world. Each time I needed Him, He was there to help me, guide me, and even spare me from death.

. . . .

"But by the grace of God I am what I am: and his grace which was bestowed upon me was not in vain; but I laboured more abundantly than they all: yet not I, but the grace of God which was with me." (1 Corinthians 15:10)

During a men's spiritual retreat in Southern California, I was inspired to exhort the men to strive for and attain great spiritual power. A brother was preaching about the great miracles that the disciples of Jesus had witnessed and done. As he was preaching, the Spirit came on me and led me to say, "All these miracles belong to us as well. If we are willing to work like those of old, God will bless us in the same manner."

Just then, a brother stood up and said, "Thus sayeth the Lord! All of these can be yours."

I understood that day what the apostle Paul was saying in his letter to the Corinthians. If I were to dedicate my life to serving Jesus and laboring as hard as I could—not acting like a minister only on Sundays or at the midweek service, but being genuine in my discipleship, making it my first responsibility—then He would bless me. If his Word said it, I could count on it.

> "But seek ye first the kingdom of God, and his righteousness; and all these things shall be added unto you" (Matthew 6:33).

Like all men, I have struggled to prioritize the different elements in my life, but whenever I have decided to follow God's will, I have never regretted my decision.

Shortly after I was ordained a minister, the company I worked for wanted me to relocate to Denver. My old job was ending, and the new offer was very attractive. It seemed like a no-brainer. I was ready to accept, but I decided to talk to my mentor, Brother Joe, first. I was surprised by his response. He told me that I simply couldn't move to Denver. The church in Anaheim was dependent on me, and besides, there was no church in Denver. My young ministry would go sour. He said that God would provide work for me if I stayed in California and put my ministry first.

I stayed and continued to pastor the church in Anaheim. Before I knew it, the Lord had provided me with another job. The blessings I enjoyed during this period were unprecedented.

As I continued to grow and mature, I was determined to experience everything that God was able to bless me with—in short, the infinite. As I studied the Scripture, I read about people being translated and carried into heaven without facing death, transported by the Holy Spirit from one town to another, speaking in tongues, and receiving many other miraculous visitations from God. My mentor, Brother Joe, assured me that none of these things would transpire in my life unless I gave myself entirely to Jesus. He told me that working for the Lord had to be unconditional. I could never impose a negotiation or a qualification upon it, like "Lord, I will serve you if . . ." or "God, I will obey you if . . ." I realized it is much simpler than that. When the Lord says, "Follow me," the nets have to be dropped. The incident with the rental car attendant taught me that disobedience was bitter, and obedience brought spiritual exhilaration.

I would now like to share that spiritual exhilaration. The next part of this book is a collection of miracles and experiences that I have directly witnessed. They are sometimes grouped in categories, and they are in no chronological order. My purpose in sharing them is to draw people closer to God and show them His matchless power.

PART TWO

GOING OUT

MIRACLES TAKE FLIGHT

And Jesus came and spake unto them, saying, All
power is given unto me in heaven and in earth. Go
ye therefore, and teach all nations, baptizing them
in the name of the Father, and of the Son, and
of the Holy Ghost. Teaching them to observe all
things whatsoever I have commanded you: and,
lo, I am with you always, even unto the end of the
world. Amen.

—Matthew 28:18-20

It was a beautiful summer afternoon in Orange County,
California—a perfect day for flying. Caryl and I were
waiting in line to board an airplane that was going to
take us to Pittsburgh for a weeklong church retreat. We flew
out of the John Wayne airport. While standing in line, Caryl
began playing with a small Mexican baby who was on his
mother's shoulders in front of her.

The plane was full, and we were sitting close to the back.
Upon takeoff, I immediately fell asleep. I was wakened by
an announcement made over the plane's public address
system. The flight attendant was asking if there was a doctor
on board. I rubbed my eyes and looked down the long aisle
to see a flight attendant kneeling on the floor, administering
oxygen to that same little baby Caryl had been playing with
earlier.

Without hesitation, I got out of my seat and began walking toward the baby. I knew what needed to be done. As I approached the attendant, she asked, "Are you a doctor?"

"No," I replied.

She commanded, "Go back to your seat. This is an emergency, and I am losing this baby."

She was right. As I examined the baby with my eyes, I saw that his little body was rigid, and his face had already turned blue from lack of oxygen. I said to her in a calm voice, "I am a minister of the Lord Jesus Christ, and I am going to pray for this baby, and he will be all right."

I then turned to the mother and told her in Spanish that I was a minister and that I wanted to pray for her baby. With huge tears running down her cheeks, she cried out, "*Si! Si, por favor.*"

I took the baby in my hands and was shocked as I lifted him up. He was as stiff as a board. I stood him on his mother's lap, took the blessed oil out of my pocket, and placed a small drop on his head. Just as I was going to lay my hands on the baby's head, I heard a man near me mutter, "What is this fool going to do?"

When I think back on it, I probably did not look like a man of God, whatever a man of God looks like. I was dressed very casually, and I had been sleeping, so my rumpled clothing and tousled hair must have made me look like I had just rolled out of bed. But I proceeded anyhow. I could feel my knees beginning to weaken as everyone on the plane stared at me. After a moment of heart-fluttering silence, I managed to push all the negative thoughts out of my mind. I laid my hands on the child's head and said the worst prayer of my life. I said it out loud for all to hear me. "God, you made this kid, and you know what is wrong with him. In the name of Jesus, fix him." How elegant.

I turned and walked back to my seat, where Caryl and the young lady next to her were praying and crying. I sat for a moment with closed eyes and thanked God for his mercy. When I opened my eyes, I saw the little child standing on his seat, facing backwards, with his chin on the headrest. He was looking directly into my eyes. He had a huge smile on his face as if to say, "Thank you." I praised God for His mercy.

There was another incident in an airplane that was very powerful and produced a healing of a different sort. I had boarded my flight in Phoenix on an excruciatingly hot summer day. The temperature was well over 100 degrees, and the inside of the plane was getting hotter with every person who boarded. I was in an aisle seat, and the one next to me was empty. I was praying that it stayed that way. A beautiful young lady boarded. She was dressed very nicely and carried a blue book held tightly in her arms against her chest. Her face indicated that something was dreadfully wrong. She sat next to me, and it was apparent that she had been crying.

I tried to break the ice by asking her what a beautiful young lady should be so concerned about. I thought for a second, and then I added that I hoped she didn't take that the wrong way. I told her that I was a minster, and maybe I could help.

Then this young woman erupted. Tears and emotion accompanied a story about a father who had left his wife and daughter when she was one year old. Of course, she was that daughter who had been abandoned and forgotten for many years. As it turned out, her father was now in a sanitarium, struggling with several health issues, including alcoholism—hence, the big blue book (*Alcoholics Anonymous*) she was carrying. We were leveling off as she continued to describe her hate for this man and what it had done to her mom. This young woman's name was Linda.

When Linda took a breath, God stepped in. I said to her, "How can you ever love your husband and your two boys the way they deserve to be loved while carrying all of this anger and hate in your heart?"

She responded in shock, "I didn't tell you that I had two boys."

"No, but God did," I said, "and He wants to help you."

Linda was so astonished at this revelation that she quieted and began to listen. I admonished her and said, "First, you have to make yourself right with God and ask for forgiveness for your thoughts and actions. I will pray for you now, but you have to repent, and I can't do that for you."

We joined hands, and I offered prayer. I asked God to allow the spirit of repentance to fall on her. After praying, I launched into Prayer 101. She was taken aback by the simplicity of my directions. I told her that she should take some private time that night to kneel down and ask God to take away her hate and fill her heart with love for her father.

By this time, we were landing. I gave her my phone number and the address to the church if she needed any more help. We parted, and frankly, I forgot about the incident.

The following Sunday, during the break between Sunday school and the morning worship service, one of the deacons came to me and said that there was a young lady in the sanctuary looking for me. I told Caryl that it might be Linda and asked her to come with me to meet her. As I walked up to Linda, she embraced me. Tears were streaming down her cheeks. When I asked her what had happened, she could barely talk.

She sobbed as she relayed the events of the night after our flight together. She told me how she had gone into the bathroom and knelt by the bathtub to pray. She said that she could barely find the words to say, but she asked the Lord to take the burden from her heart so that she could be a better wife and mother. She asked the Lord to fill the emptiness with love. Then she said, "John, He did. He did it for me. All of the pain is gone. All of the hurt is gone. My husband told me that I should ask Dad to come and live with us. My boys are so excited that their grandpa is coming to be with us. How can I ever thank you?"

"Don't thank me," I said. "Just praise and honor the Lord Jesus Christ. He did it for you. He loved you so much that He died on the cross just for you and for sinners like me."

· · · ·

The next several years were filled with airplane miracles. It's often said that people are more likely to open up on airplanes for one reason or another. Maybe it's because of the close proximity that we have with one another—constantly invading private space, accidentally touching elbows, and knocking knees. Maybe we spill our guts because we believe we will probably never see the person again, so what difference does it make if he or she knows our secrets? Or maybe it is due to the little subconscious fear we all have when we think too hard about being confined to pressurized tubes soaring well above the earth's atmosphere. We can each believe what we want, but I always try to take advantage of my captive audience and am always ready when the Lord prompts.

Over the years, I have anointed flight attendants for cancer, women with emotional scars, people with nervous disorders, fear-filled children, and even a pregnant woman who was afraid to tell her husband that she had conceived. Each time, I have tested God to ensure that the anointing was His will and not mine.

Once, while waiting in the gate area, God pointed out a young lady in need of prayer. I said silently in my heart, "Lord, that woman may feel it's inappropriate for me to walk up to her and ask if I can pray for her. Have her sit next to me when we board the plane." God never fails. She did.

Sometimes those that I meet on planes only introduce ourselves to one another by giving first names, and other times, we share business cards. Most of the time, I never hear from them again, and that is okay with me. I have e-mailed back and forth with some a few times. Then one of us either gives up or forgets. But every time, the person receives. He or she receives, because Christ has infinite love and compassion for the people He created. He proved it to us by giving His perfect life in exchange for our sinful one.

"Greater love hath no man than this, that a man lay down his life for his friends" (John 15:13).

Christ has given us the ability to once again enter into the presence of the Father as we did so freely when we were children. He gave us the opportunity to be born again—not of the flesh, but of the Spirit. Through His death and resurrection, He gave us the ability to become sons and daughters of God.

CASTING OUT DEVILS

Sister Barbara was diagnosed with terminal cancer, and even though the entire church was praying, her prognosis looked bleak. Several days after she was admitted to the hospital, word reached us that Sister Barbara had seen a vision of an angel standing by her bedside. Normally this would be supremely comforting, but I trembled when I heard that the angel was supposedly wearing a brown coat. I had never heard of an angel wearing a dark, sad color before.

Every week, I would take communion to Sister Barbara and spend some time at her bedside. One particular week, I was stricken with a kidney stone and ended up in the hospital myself. If you've ever experienced the pain caused by a kidney stone, you'll believe me when I say that I was a complete mess.

After I was discharged from the hospital in a delicate state, my daughter and wife nursed me back to health, although the stone had not yet passed. One evening, I felt well enough to go to the hospital and administer the Lord's Supper to Sister Barbara. My wife drove, and as we got closer to the hospital, I started to feel a little uncomfortable. As we entered the hospital and walked the long corridors to her room, my pain increased. It felt like a long three-sided dagger was being twisted into my back. By the time I reached her bedside, I was about to pass out.

Sister Barbara, who was in and out of a coma, looked at me and said simply, "He is going to destroy you."

"Who is?"

"He is going to destroy you. He is standing over there in the corner, laughing."

By that time, my knees were giving way, and I was covered in a cold sweat. I asked my wife to get me out of there. She helped me to the car, and I asked her to take me to our mission in Santa Ana, because they had Tuesday evening meetings, and I needed the ministry to pray for me.

We entered the church, and the elders put oil on my head and then prayed for me. When they finished, a sister in the congregation stood and said that she had a vision. She saw a light come down from heaven and rest upon me while the ministry was praying.

I felt like a new man. The pain departed, and I could walk. I asked Caryl to drive me home, but she hesitated and then began to cry. She said that we needed to go and help our Sister Barbara. I acquiesced, but hesitantly. I didn't want to go back into the presence of that questionable angel, but I also knew that I couldn't leave Sister Barbara in his hands either. To my surprise, Caryl began to tell me about a dream she had a few nights before. In the dream, Sister Barbara was alone and forsaken by everybody. Caryl said, "We have to go back and help her." I knew that she was right.

As we parked the car in the visitor's parking lot, the Spirit of God began building inside me. We entered the hospital, and something amazing began to happen. Somehow, we were no longer walking under our own power. We were being carried in the Spirit. Lifted off the ground, we floated down a long hallway and into an elevator. No sooner had the doors to the elevator shut than they opened again, and we were on the eighth floor. Both of us felt an extraordinary power carrying us toward our destination.

As Caryl and I approached Sister Barbara's room, we both felt a strong cold, wind blow upon us. After we entered into the room, I fell to my knees and began to pray. The Spirit poured out of me as I rebuked the evil presence in the name of Jesus.

When I finished praying, I stood and leaned on the bedrail. Tears began to roll from Sister Barbara's eyes. After a while, she began to sing.

When peace like a river attendeth my way
When sorrows like sea billows roll
What ever my lot thou hast taught me to say.
It is well, it is well with my soul.

It Is Well With My Soul, Horation B. Spafford

Caryl and I joined Sister Barbara in finishing the song. Then she opened her eyes and said to me, "He fled. He is gone. He ran out of the room as you entered."

We rejoiced together for a while, and then I administered to her the bread and the wine representing the flesh and blood of Jesus Christ.

A few days later, Sister Barbara was released from the hospital. She called me and asked if I could come to her home for a visit. When I arrived, she showed me a large box of prescription drugs. She said that the morning after I prayed for her, the attending physician came to check on her. After looking at her chart, he went ballistic and demanded to know who prescribed all the medications—the medications in the box—that eventually put Sister Barbara in a drug-induced coma.

No one took responsibility, of course, and the man in the brown coat was nowhere to be found.

· · · ·

And they came over unto the other side of the sea, into the country of the Gadarenes. And when he was come out of the ship, immediately there met him out of the tombs a man with an unclean spirit, Who had his dwelling among the tombs; and no man could bind him, no, not with chains: Because that he had been often bound with fetters and chains, and the chains had been plucked asunder by him, and the fetters broken in pieces: neither could any man tame him. And always, night and day, he was in the mountains, and in the tombs, crying, and cutting himself with stones. But when he saw Jesus afar off, he ran and worshipped him, And cried with a loud voice, and said, What have I to do with thee, Jesus, thou Son of the most high God? I adjure thee by God, that thou torment me not. For he said unto him, Come out of the man, thou unclean spirit. (Mark 5:1-8)

In our very modern times, we don't often hear about unclean spirits possessing people's bodies—except in horror films laden with spooky special effects, perhaps. People don't cluck their tongues at the mentally ill or even people with mild mental disorders and say that they "have a devil." When we hear about mass murderers or serial killers on the news, nobody is ever bold enough to suggest that these people are possessed by Satan. Instead, psychologists tell us about their childhoods, their medical histories, and the other factors that contributed to the making of a monster.

In our very modern world, we prefer to create names for these afflictions, discover their physical roots, and create medicines to control them—but not cure them completely. But back when Christ and his disciples walked the earth, they said that these people were possessed with unclean spirits. Even diseases such as blindness, dumbness, and epilepsy were thought to have been caused by Satan. The story of Legion, is one of the most well-known examples from Scripture, but all of the gospels—especially Luke's—are full of stories about people being healed through the expulsion of demons.

The Scriptures also tell us that casting out demons is not a business we should take lightly, and it's certainly not for the faint of heart. In fact, Acts 19 shows us that there is grave danger associated with these dealings if people don't take them seriously. In this story, seven men tried to emulate the apostle Paul in order to gain a reputation like his; however, as we read this account, it is apparent they lacked the authority needed to garner the acclaim they sought.

> Then certain of the vagabond Jews, exorcists, took
> upon them to call over them which had evil spirits
> the name of the Lord Jesus, saying, We adjure you

by Jesus whom Paul preacheth. And there were seven sons of one Sceva, a Jew, and chief of the priests, which did so. And the evil spirit answered and said, Jesus I know, and Paul I know; but who are ye? And the man in whom the evil spirit was leaped on them, and overcame them, and prevailed against them, so that they fled out of that house naked and wounded. (Acts 19:13-16)

When Jesus sent His disciples out, He gave them power over these spirits. That same power is still available to us today.

Behold, I give unto you power to tread on serpents and scorpions, and over all the power of the enemy: and nothing shall by any means hurt you. Not withstanding in this rejoice not, that the spirits are subject unto you; but rather rejoice, because your names are written in heaven. (Luke 10:19-20)

The Scriptures tell us that God never changes. Therefore, if God, Christ, and the Holy Spirit are the same today as they were back then, we should expect to witness events associated with demonic spirits, even in our sophisticated society.

Caryl and I were driving through Cleveland, and the Spirit kept telling me to stop at the home of a brother and sister in Loraine. We knew this couple well, but I had not heard that there was anything wrong or anyone sick in their household. I gave in to the Spirit's urging, and we stopped at their home for the evening. After dinner, Caryl and I sat in the living room, visiting with our brother and sister, when a strange question popped out of my mouth.

"How long have you been suffering from terrible nightmares?" I asked my sister.

Not knowing exactly what her reaction would be to this off-the-wall question, I watched as a look of surprise slowly covered her face. I could tell she wasn't exactly shocked by my question. Her expression had too much stress mixed in with the surprise. She pressed her lips together tightly, and her forehead became a maze of mountains and valleys. Apparently, this issue—just like all nagging, lurking fears—was constantly bubbling just below the surface of my sister's pleasant countenance.

Understanding that the Lord was the only one who could have revealed this to me, my sister began to explain the terrible dreams she was having each night. "Sometimes I feel that someone or something is actually in my home, and I'm gripped with fear. Sometimes the dreams are so real, I wake up in the middle of the night and can't go back to sleep. It's not a fear that goes away once the dreams are over. It stays with me. It's almost like I've been traumatized by these things. I can't stop thinking about them, even when the sun is shining brightly and I'm going about my daily routine."

I let this sister get it all out of her system before I did anything. After she was finished, we all got on our knees to pray for God's power. I then offered to pray for her. I laid my hands on the top of her head and prayed that God would expel the spirit that was causing her so much grief.

We retired for the night, but Caryl and I kept praying. When we emerged for breakfast the next morning, we could both see the difference in our sister's face. The joy of Christ was shining through her countenance, and the fear was gone.

. . . .

Caryl and I were friends with a couple who were heavily interested in martial arts. They enjoyed the physical and mental stamina, strength, and control that they gained from their training. They exercised five days a week and regularly competed in tournaments and other events. It was more than a hobby for them. It shaped their lifestyle.

One evening, Caryl and I were enjoying dinner with this couple at an outdoor restaurant. We weren't far into our conversation before I found myself saying to my friend's wife, "Tell me about your nightmares."

She paused a moment, and I could tell she was trying to remember if she had ever told Caryl or me about the bad dreams, because as far as she was concerned, the only person who knew was her husband. Her eyes darted from side to side, looking for someone who might jump in and rescue her from the turn our conversation had taken.

I tried to regain her focus by saying, "Please. I know about the nightmares. If you tell me about them, maybe I can help you."

She relented. "I have the same dream every night. I know before I go to bed that I'm going to have the dream. I dread falling asleep, because I know that instead of waking up feeling rested and recharged, I'm going to wake up in a cold sweat because of the dream."

"What do you see in your dream?"

"When I explain it to you, it won't even sound that bad. In the dream, I always see the same hideous personage. It's hard to describe why he's so frightening. He is ugly, but it's not his ugliness that scares me. It's the feeling that I get when I see him. I know that he wants to cause me harm. In the dream, he is always trying to steal my daughter."

"Are you having the same dreams?" I asked her husband.

He nodded, dazed by each word being said. He proceeded to describe the ugly personage in detail. He concluded by adding, "Somehow, I don't think of it as a dream. I feel like it's real—like that thing is real—that he is somehow really affecting our daughter. I can't describe it, but it's not like a normal dream. I can't think about it like I do other, ordinary dreams."

We finished our dinner and went back to their home. Even though I didn't know much about martial arts myself, I felt I should share a thought that came to my mind. From what I understood, beginners in martial arts start by mastering the physical exercises and routines. As they continue, they develop mental stamina and accuracy of movements. Those who choose to continue further enter a sort of spiritual training. I explained that entering into the spiritual realm outside of the protection of Christ was very dangerous.

As I was talking, I saw a change come over their faces. I noticed that they weren't looking at me any longer. They seemed to be looking through me at something just beyond where I was standing. I got their attention again by asking if they would like me to pray for them. They both agreed swiftly. When I finished the prayer, I felt a cold wind pass over me, and I knew that something evil had exited the house.

My friend's wife stood and said calmly, "Before you prayed, while you were talking to us, I saw the hideous personage appear in the window behind you."

"I saw it, too," her husband said just as calmly, rising to stand next to her.

She continued, "While you were praying for us, I kept looking at the figure in the window. As you prayed, the figure slowly vanished."

My friends were never bothered again.

. . . .

Caryl and I were friends with another couple who had a similar experience. They were at the gym one morning when my friend's wife had a seizure. After being taken to the hospital, she was given the frightening news that they had found a mysterious tumor on her brain.

I was in California on business, so as soon as I got word of what had happened, I rushed to the hospital to see her. When I arrived in her room, the surgeon was talking with her and her husband. I could hear the surgeon speculating about what they might have to do. I caught phrases like "drill a hole in your skull," "extensive recovery," and other snippets that could only be describing possible side effects of such an operation. The surgeon's bedside manner was poor, and by the time he finished, I could see panic and fear written all over my friend's face.

When the surgeon left, I walked to my friend's bedside, and one of the beatitudes came to my mind:

"Blessed are the pure of heart for they shall see God" (Matthew 5:8).

When I said this verse aloud, she looked up at me in a kind of stupor. The doctors had already given her anti-seizure medications. This, along with the fear she was undoubtedly feeling, had knocked her into an altered state of consciousness. I found myself boldly stating that she would not need to have an operation but that God was going take this away from her. Then I anointed and prayed for her, for I truly felt that she was *pure of heart.*

My friend's husband asked if I would come to their home that night rather than stay at a hotel. I agreed. While we were having coffee, he told me of some very strange things that had been going on in their home. He said that often in the middle of the night, they would hear a tapping noise against the wall. Thinking it was their German Shepherd wagging his tail against the wall, he would get up and find the dog sleeping well away from where the noise was coming from. But even stranger than that, he said that as they were preparing to go to the gym that morning, his wife had urgently called him into the bathroom. He was shocked to see that smoke was coming out of her mouth as she breathed.

When I heard these things, I knew that we were not wrestling against *flesh and blood*. We were struggling with an evil spirit.

In the course of the next few weeks, my friend went through many scans and tests. The doctors said the object did not look like a tumor but more like a parasite. They could try killing it with surgery or shrinking it with medications.

One day, I was out for a long run, deep in prayer for my friend while my feet pounded the sidewalk. Suddenly, I had an impulse to look up at the sky, and I was stunned by what I saw. The clouds above me had formed into the shape of a huge angel, possibly a mile tall and so detailed that I simply could not stop staring at him. *This is what an archangel must look like,* I thought. In the place where his face should have been, there was a gap in the clouds, and the sun blazed through in a fiery beam. I knew immediately that God was hearing our prayers and that He was going to answer them. But the battle was not over.

Shortly after this, I returned to California for business. I asked my friend and his wife to come to my hotel for prayer. I had also asked another minister to join me. We were all going to meet at my hotel near the airport. When the shuttle dropped me off at the front entrance of the hotel, I noticed my minister friend sitting in his car. I went to the car and asked him why he didn't go inside the lobby, where he could have waited comfortably. He told me that the power of evil was so strong he could not get out of his vehicle.

Here we go, I thought. When the couple arrived, we went up to my room, read some Scripture, and got on our knees to pray. When we finished, my minister friend and I anointed my friend again, this time with the understanding that we were working against an evil spirit. We felt the power of God during our prayer, so we rejoiced. Then we all retired to the hotel's restaurant, where we had planned to eat dinner together.

We were laughing and enjoying one another's company when I noticed that across the room, there was a man sitting alone. He looked at me and sneered. His countenance was distorted. I knew it was evil. I didn't say anything to my friends. The man kept glaring at me.

When my friends and I were saying our good-byes, my friend turned to me and asked, "Did you see him, too—the evil one, sitting alone?"

"The man in the dining room? Yes, I saw him. But he won't bother your wife any longer." To myself, I thought, *I am sure that he and I will meet again.*

Shortly after our meeting at the hotel, my friend's wife began to heal without the aid of surgery or medications. The scans showed that the parasite was dissolving—apparently all on its own!

. . . .

"And lest I should be exalted above measure
through the abundance of the revelations,
there was given to me a thorn in the flesh, the

messenger of Satan to buffet me, lest I should be exalted above measure." (2 Corinthians 12:7)

I was just about to return home from a missionary trip to the Philippines when I experienced my second kidney stone. Kidney stones may be Satan's weapon of choice for me—I don't know—but the pain that they cause is excruciating. I was the first of the missionaries to depart, and while we were all on our knees, praying for my safe return, stabbing pain flared through my torso. There it was—the three-sided dagger being twisted into my back.

My missionary partners were worried about me traveling home alone. One of them suggested the rest of them cut off the last bit of the mission trip so that we could all travel together. I knew what was going on, and I was not going to be the cause of bringing this trip to an early end.

I had the brothers anoint me and pray for me before they saw me off to the airport. The bumpy ride to Davao City exacerbated the pain so greatly that I asked the brothers to pray for me again en route. When we arrived, I asked the brothers to anoint me one last time. We all knew that Satan wanted to interrupt the trip. He knew that many souls were going to give themselves to the Lord, and he was going to try to frustrate and stall our efforts any way that he could.

I convinced the brothers that I would be okay once I got on the plane. They called the States and spread the word that I was having physical problems, knowing that many of the saints would pray for me. One elderly couple, Brother Jim and Sister Mary, were eating dinner when they received the call. Brother Jim was another of my mentors and an apostle in the church. He immediately asked his wife to join him as he knelt to pray for me. While they were praying, Brother Jim had a vision in which he saw a man dressed all in white walk up behind me and place his hand on my back. He knew immediately that I would be all right.

Oblivious to anything except the pain in my back, I took my seat on the big 747—thankfully in the exit row. Glorious legroom! Sighing in relief, I turned to greet the man on my right, and to my shock, it was the Devil.

His face, like the face of the man I had seen in the restaurant, was contorted and disfigured. He sneered at me in an aloof manner but would not acknowledge me. I couldn't believe it! I was going to sit next to the Devil on a four-hour flight from Davao to Manila.

Knowing I had no choice, I sat and waited for takeoff. As soon as the flight attendants pressurized the cabin, the pain increased beyond anything I had ever known. Immediately when the seat belt sign clicked off, I got up and bounced like a pinball down the aisle toward the restroom. In that cramped compartment, I knelt in prayer.

When I finished, I forced my shaky legs to take me back to my seat, but as soon as I slumped down next to the Devil, the pain escalated in a matter of seconds. Sweat gathered under my shirt and behind my knees. I stood up in the aisle, steadied myself, began the long trek back to the restroom, and fell to my knees in prayer once again. On my third trip back to the restroom, I was determined not to get up until God heard me. This time, I was not necessarily praying for a healing; I was praying that God would rebuke the evil spirit from that man and from our plane. I prayed fervently and ended my prayer with the realization that the satanic being had no business on our plane.

I said, "Lord, tell this evil spirit that he can leave this man now, because he failed to stop our missionary trip. He doesn't need to hang around. Please command him to leave."

When I finally made my way back to my seat, I curled up and closed my eyes. Without warning, I heard the plane's emergency door open and bang shut. A frightened flight attendant came running up the aisle and just stared at the door. I knew that he had heard it, too. God was establishing the truth with two witnesses. The flight attendant checked the door and all the latches. It was locked and secured but there was no question of what we both heard. God had allowed us to hear the sound that the door would make if opened as evidence that he had ejected Satan from the man next to me.

As for my pain, it subsided immediately, and the man next to me turned toward me with a face that was completely changed. He was smiling and turned out to be a very nice person. We talked for the remaining portion of our trip.

OVERCOME OBSTACLES

Things were going well in the job God had given me. One day at work, a young lady came to my office and asked to talk to me. She was an account manager whom I had seen around the office and in meetings. She sat down gently in the chair opposite my desk and began to say something extraordinary. "Yesterday, when we were attending the sales presentation, I looked at you and saw a light surrounding your head. I know I must sound crazy, and I am confused by what I saw, but I felt like I was being directed to talk to you." She paused for several seconds and then said something that made my bones go cold. "I have been considering suicide."

"Why?" I asked.

"I've been living with the same man for eight years. We have a six-year old daughter, and I always thought that he would marry me eventually. Recently he told me that he . . . didn't think it was going to work out. He broke it off, and my daughter and I moved into an apartment. I'm trying to be strong for her, but I'm . . . I'm devastated. I can't face my family. They warned me so many times that this would happen. I don't know what to do."

Flabbergasted, I stared into the tortured face of the young account manager. I offered to pray for her and explained the process of laying on of hands and the anointing of oil. She was not open to it but I asked her to read James 5:14 that evening.

The next day was Good Friday, and the company where I worked was scheduled to close at noon. About 10:00 AM this troubled young lady came into my office and closed the door behind her. She said, "Go ahead and anoint me. I read the Scripture last night. I understand."

When I did, I simply asked God to give her the strength to overcome the obstacles she was facing.

That evening was the start of our Easter weekend, and I was so busy with guests and Easter services that I confess I forgot all about her need. When I returned to work the following Monday, I couldn't believe that I had neglected to call her and hoped she had not done anything foolish. As I was standing in our office lobby, she came in and made a beeline for me.

Her eyes were already moist when she said, "When I woke up on Sunday morning, I was so depressed that I just sat on the edge of my bed, planning how I would kill myself. I was staring out my window at the ocean when all of a sudden—I can't explain this part except to just tell you what I saw. I saw a hill with three crosses on it. I knew that I should be looking at ocean, but I saw the hill with three crosses instead. Then—John, I know that you of all people will believe me when I say that a voice spoke to me. It said, 'Go on with your life; I have given you the strength to overcome these obstacles.' The desire to take my life completely left me. Now I know that I can go forward. I can live my life without this man. There is someone much greater who is a part of my life now."

The significance of these and many other miracles are for the glorification of God and His Son Jesus Christ. These experiences urge people to work at establishing a relationship with Him, just as this young account manager did that day.

AND CHILDREN ARE GIVEN

n the Book of 2 Kings, there is a story of the prophet Elisha promising an elderly woman a child.

> And he said, "What then is to be done for her?"

> And Gehazi answered, "Verily she hath no child, and her husband is old."

> And he said, "Call her." And when he had called her, she stood in the door. And he said, "About this season, according to the time of life, thou shalt embrace a son."

> And she said, "Nay, my lord, thou man of God, do not lie unto thine handmaid."

> And the woman conceived, and bare a son at that season that Elisha had said unto her, according to the time of life. (2 Kings 4:14-17)

It's amazing how many infertile women populate the Scriptures. Abraham's wife, Sarah, was barren until she conceived Isaac at ninety years old. Elizabeth bore John the Baptist after her physical body denied the possibility. And, of course, there was Hannah, Samuel's mother.

Knowing of these things and how they transpired builds our faith.

"So then faith cometh by hearing, and hearing by the word of God" (Romans 10:17).

The Word of God enters our minds and stays alive. It resonates in our hearts and in our spirits. It is there when we have a need.

Once, Caryl and I were attending a missionary meeting in Youngstown, Ohio, and we felt we should ask a young couple if we could stay the night at their home. They were happy to receive us, and while we were fellowshipping together, the husband told us that they had been trying to have children. As it turned out, he and his wife had been through several miscarriages, and they had grown discouraged. As he was talking, I remembered Hannah's prayer found in the first chapter of 1 Samuel, which describes how discouraged she had become.

When the husband finished telling us their story, I asked if we could anoint his wife. We all knelt in prayer and then anointed our young sister with the blessed oil. We poured out our hearts to God in unison on our sister's behalf. Then we all retired for the evening.

I was getting comfortable in bed when a bolt of lightning filled the house with a bright light and thunder boomed. Caryl ran out of the bathroom and asked, "What was that?"

We both looked out the window and saw a cloudless sky and the frozen snow covering the ground. I turned to Caryl and said, "God heard our prayers. Cindy will have a child."

Cindy now has three children, and her life is filled with joy.

This same type of situation has happened five times now. Some of my friends refer to me as the *fertility* minister in jest. But I don't really care how they refer to me as long as God hears my prayers and comes to the rescue of those discouraged sisters who believe that He is the same today as He was then.

MOVING MOUNTAINS

And Jesus said unto them, Because of your
unbelief: for verily I say unto you, If ye have faith
as a grain of mustard seed, ye shall say unto this
mountain, Remove hence to yonder place; and
it shall remove; and nothing shall be impossible
unto you.

—Matthew 17:20

These words remind us that if we exhibit even the
smallest amount of faith, we can move mountains.
Most of the time, we interpret the word "mountains"
in this Scripture to mean large trials in our lives. But I
always thought it was interesting that Jesus was talking
about literally moving mountains in addition to the larger
metaphor His teaching represents. Sometimes I try and
imagine what it would be like to see a mountain move—not
to mention trying to imagine the circumstances in which I
would *need* to move a mountain. In all my years of ministry,
I have never seen a mountain actually move, but this next
story comes close in that it defies all the physical laws of the
universe.

Just a few years ago, I was in Italy for missionary work.
I found myself traveling north on the *autostrada* to Rome
after a beautiful series of meetings in Calabria. Rosario,
the minister of our Italian mission, was behind the wheel,
speeding along at a nauseating ninety-five miles per hour.
Although Rosario fulfilled each and every stereotype that
Americans have about crazy Italian drivers, I had traveled

these roads with him for fifteen years, and I had no concerns about his ability to get us to Rome.

We both felt relieved when we left the mountains of southern Italy, whose twisty roads comprise the most difficult part of the trip. As we rounded a bend, we saw that there was road construction ahead. A sign indicated that we had to cross over the median and drive on the opposite side of the road as the four-lane highway was reduced to two lanes.

As Rosario began to cross over the median, the car hit a cement center divider that was angled upward. Instead of coming to a crushing stop, the angle of the median catapulted our vehicle into the air. My stomach lurched as I realized we were going to crash into oncoming traffic. When I try to replay these few moments in slow motion, I remember that we were flying over the center divider, which was at least three feet high, and we were about to collide head-on with a truck. I remember thinking, "Lord, please help us! If you don't, we are going to die."

What happened next is the part that defies the laws of nature. In an instant, we were moved about thirty feet to the right of the center divider and placed on a flat surface of the closed portion of the road that had not yet been demolished. I cannot describe it in any other way, and I cannot offer any concrete explanation as to how we landed in safety other than to shout with all of my heart that it was God's merciful hand.

Rosario and I both sat for a moment in silence. We knew that what we had just experienced was impossible. Our minds were already trying to rationalize it. What could have possibly caused a 2,500-pound car flying at more than forty miles an hour to suddenly switch directions in midair? What kind of air pocket or gust of wind could have moved our car and then deposited it on the other side of the road?

When we came to our senses, Rosario got out of the car and began to shout, *"E un miracolo! E un miracolo, gloria a Dio!"*

It was a miracle to us—something that no human being could have done for us or any law of nature could have arranged—but it was a cinch to the living God. It was easy as pie for the Lord Jesus Christ, who told his disciples not to worry about their well-being, for if God feeds the birds and clothes the lilies, He will certainly care for those who follow Him.

Let me emphasize that God alone gets the credit for this event. He spared us from a terrible accident that could have taken our lives or done irreparable damage to our bodies. God didn't do this because we were really great Christians. He didn't do it to reward us for our service. He did it because He loves His children and chose to be merciful, plain and simple.

IN THE SPIRIT ON THE LORD'S DAY

I was in the Spirit on the Lord's day, and heard
behind me a great voice, as of a trumpet

—Revelation 1:10.

The Holy Spirit is a gift from God that resides within us after we accept Christ and are baptized. When we want to communicate with God, the best possibility of ensuring His response is to be *in the Spirit* ourselves. This sounds simple enough, right? But what does it mean to be in the Spirit? If the Spirit is inside us, wouldn't we be in the Spirit all the time? Not necessarily. We can squash God's Spirit into silence if we crowd our soul with ungodly input. When we obey Christ's commandments and keep our souls pure, we allow the Spirit room to grow within us. When the Spirit is enlarged and encouraged to work, then we are more likely to be in the Spirit.

While I knew all this, I wanted to truly understand it. One evening, while on a business trip, I lay on the bed in my hotel room, reading the first chapter of Revelation. The apostle John had been banished to the Island of Patmos by the Roman emperor Domitian around AD 95. The island was used for prisoners, and they had no rights. But John didn't see that as a problem. He saw it as an opportunity to speak to God and receive revelation.

I John, who also am your brother, and companion
in tribulation, and in the kingdom and patience of
Jesus Christ, was in the isle that is called Patmos,

for the word of God, and for the testimony of Jesus Christ. I was in the Spirit on the Lord's day, and heard behind me a great voice, as of a trumpet, Saying, I am Alpha and Omega, the first and the last. (Revelation 1:9-11)

After reading this, I sat back on the bed for a moment and wondered what John meant when he said that he was *in the Spirit on the Lord's day.* Why did the writers capitalize Spirit, and what did it feel like to be in the Spirit?

As I meditated, a wonderful thing happened to me. I found myself floating effortlessly toward the ceiling of the hotel room. I wasn't afraid. In fact, I remember thinking, *How cool is this?* As I approached the ceiling, I was going to push myself back and see if I would float upward again, as though I were an astronaut in zero gravity.

To my surprise, I passed through the ceiling without feeling a thing. I then found myself soaring over the desert and then over the mountains. I could see the little remaining snow on the highest elevations of the Colorado Rockies. *I was in the Spirit,* and it was exhilarating. A few moments passed in which I purely enjoyed the ride.

Then I began to actually think about what was happening to me. Why was I flying? Where was I? How was I going to return? The moment these thoughts entered my mind, I was placed immediately back into my body. There I was, in my hotel room, on the bed where I had been reading. I realized that God had answered my question and showed me what it was like to be in the Spirit. I admit that I tried to duplicate this event, but I was not able to do it with my own power. Only the Lord could make that happen. I had not controlled what had just happened; He had. Then I realized why the *s* in the word "Spirit" was capitalized. It signifies the Spirit as part of the Godhead, representing the mind and the will of the Father and the Son.

. . . .

During the first couple of energetic years when I was studying excessively, new questions would arise in my mind, and God would answer me. I believe He did this because He knew that I sincerely wanted to understand Him and His ways to the best of my ability. I wanted to ensure that I was doing His will. Through this period of obsessive study, I recognized that the deeper I got into the Word, the more spiritual activity I experienced. It is written that the early apostles studied for six days without eating or drinking, being satisfied and filled with the indwelling of the Word. Moses stayed on the mountain with God for forty days at a time without eating or drinking, again being sustained by the Spirit of God.

The year following our baptisms, Caryl and I decided to study the Scriptures in depth. We read the Scriptures constantly. In fact, for my fortieth birthday, we obtained a time-share in Madonna di Campiglio, Italy and spent the better part of two weeks there, reading and discussing Scripture most of the day.

We went to Italy to *study Scripture?* It may not sound like fun, but let me paint a picture of what it was like. We were in the mountains of northern Italy, and the scenery was breathtaking. Traveling there, we saw picturesque alpine villages nestled in the spiky green hills. Caryl and I would take walks around the little town where we stayed, breathing in the fresh air. The days were quiet, and time passed luxuriously slowly. Our timeshare was actually a little flat. We would snuggle up to one another and read out loud and to ourselves. We would cook for each other and then read some more. It was glorious. Even though it isn't exactly how most people would picture a vacation, I remember it being one of the most peaceful and meditative trips we have ever taken.

One afternoon, Caryl said that she would really like to see this place in the winter when the mountains were dusted with pristine white snow. I said that I was having enough trouble driving on the narrow roads, and the last thing that I needed was snow to complicate things. We both chuckled, but the next morning, I awoke to the sound of Caryl's laughter.

"John! Come here, quick!" she called. As I entered the room, she was standing in her pajamas in front of the window. Behind her, to my chagrin, the craggy rocks were covered with snow.

"When I said my prayers last night," she said sheepishly, "I asked God if it were possible for me to see the Matterhorn with snow." The Lord had granted this small request, and to my joy, most of the snow melted by noon.

Those two weeks were filled with blessings, and everything seemed to go just right. On our flight back to the United States, I was reading when two ladies from Mexico approached my seat. They asked me to pray for them, and they wanted me to bring the gospel to their hometown of

Pedernales. I asked them why they would ask me to do this. I had never seen these women before.

They responded by saying, "The Spirit directed us to you."

It had nothing to do with me. If we nourish the Spirit of God within us with the Word of God, it will grow to the point where others feel it, too. When the apostle Peter walked through the streets, the sick lined up along the road, hoping to get close enough to him for a healing. His shadow had nothing to do with it. It was the Spirit of God with in him.

"Insomuch that they brought forth the sick into the streets, and laid them on beds and couches, that at the least the shadow of Peter passing by might overshadow some of them" (Acts 5:15).

FEED THE FIVE THOUSAND

But Jesus said unto them, They need not depart;
give ye them to eat. And they say unto him, We
have here but five loaves, and two fishes. He said,
Bring them hither to me. And he commanded the
multitude to sit down on the grass, and took the
five loaves, and the two fishes, and looking up
to heaven, he blessed, and brake, and gave the
loaves to his disciples, and the disciples to the
multitude. And they did all eat, and were filled:
and they took up of the fragments that remained
twelve baskets full.

—Matthew 14:16-20

I was elected to lead the world-wide missionary efforts
of our church and felt that it was my duty to visit as
many of our overseas missions as possible. In 2002 I was
preparing for one such trip to Kenya. It would be my first visit
there. As usual, the most difficult thing about preparing for
the trip was packing. After I laid out the clothing and hygiene
items that I knew would barely get me through three weeks
in a foreign land, I realized that I was going to have to *wrestle*
my suitcase shut.

One evening, I came home from work to find about six
plastic zip-sealed bags of Tootsie Pops on the kitchen table. I
called out for Caryl, asking, "What are these for?"

"They're for the kids in Kenya," she responded from
another room.

"Honey, you've got to be kidding," I called back, immediately thinking about how embarrassing it would be to lose a wrestling match with my suitcase. "You saw how full my bag is. There's no way these Tootsie Pops will fit."

"These are for the kids in Kenya," she said as she entered the room with a just-hear-me-out expression on her face. "I've heard other missionaries say that the children are very well-behaved and sit for hours while the missionaries preach. I want you to hand these out after each service as a reward for their good behavior."

"Caryl," I said in my most plaintive please-hear-*me*-out-now voice, "that's a nice idea, but these Tootsie Pops are *not* going with me to Kenya."

Of course, the Tootsie Pops went with me.

The other missionaries and I visited three to four missions a day, and at the end of each service, I passed out Tootsie Pops to the kids. It was a big hit, and just as Caryl predicted, the children truly deserved them. They sat patiently on logs or hard benches, listening tentatively, just waiting for the chance to sing for us.

On one particular visit, we were dedicating a piece of property that was going to be used to build a large facility. When I looked around, there were about thirty children in attendance. I looked in my backpack and found only twenty-three suckers in the bag. The last thing I wanted was to hurt any of the children. I told one of the other missionaries my dilemma, and he verified the count—only twenty-three suckers. He recommended that I give them to one of the Kenyan deaconesses so she could break them with her teeth and give each child a part. Hey, half a Tootsie Pop is better than no Tootsie Pop. I did what he suggested, and we proceeded with the meeting in which we dedicated the property. After the service, I saw the deaconess begin to distribute the suckers.

When we were about to leave to go to the next city, the deaconess returned the bag I had given her. I couldn't believe what I saw. There were twenty-*seven* suckers in it. I looked around and saw more than one hundred children with white sucker sticks protruding from pursed lips. We were amazed. We took pictures of the kids enjoying the treat—I knew Caryl would want to see it. She was incredibly blessed when I told her what happened. God saw her love for those kids, and He made sure that *every* child experienced that love.

Speak to the Rock

Take the rod, and gather thou the assembly together, thou, and Aaron thy brother, and speak ye unto the rock before their eyes; and it shall give forth his water, and thou shalt bring forth to them water out of the rock: so thou shalt give the congregation and their beasts drink.

—Numbers 20:8

It goes without saying that Italy is a fabulous place to do missionary work—especially on the beautiful island of Sardinia. Compared to other Third World countries where the comforts I am accustomed to aren't available, Italy is positively luxurious. When our missionary teams travel to Italy, not only are we free from worries about disease, rough travel, or the dangers of civil unrest, but we also have creature comforts such as mattresses to sleep on, temperature-controlled quarters, top-notch food, and running water. Well, we had running water every trip except one.

When we arrived in Sardinia this particular time, the brothers and sisters informed us that they were experiencing a drought. Having lived in southern California, I had experienced drought conditions before. It meant that I couldn't water my grass. In Italy, the situation was more severe. It meant that they literally ran out of water. In the area where our mission is located, the water system worked simply by gravity. There is a massive holding tank at the top of the mountain, and each home is equipped with a small tank. During a drought, the city is divided into zones, and each zone receives water on certain days of the week. If you use your tank of water before your refill day, you either have to buy more and haul it to your tank in large plastic containers or do without it.

After the Sunday service, one of the local brothers went out and banged on the water tank. It gave a sickening hollow sound. Alarmed, he removed the cover plate and was dismayed to see that there was very little water left. It was only Sunday, and the church was zoned to receive water on Thursday. With five people living in the church apartment, he knew this was going to be a serious problem.

That evening, those of us staying in the church apartment set ground rules for using the remaining water. We could all tell that it was not going to be pleasant, given the high temperatures we were experiencing and the close quarters of our accommodations.

When we retired that evening, I fell asleep before my head hit the pillow. During the day, I had preached, translated, anointed, prayed, and taught lessons. I was exhausted and began snoring loudly, which I usually do when I'm wiped out. Caryl knew she would never get to sleep with the racket I was making, so she decided that if she couldn't sleep, she would get on her knees and pray. As she was praying, she asked God to take care of the water situation. She boldly asked for a sign from God to show that He heard her. When she made that request, I immediately stopped snoring. She happily climbed in bed and fell asleep.

The next morning, I awoke first and went for a walk on the church grounds. As I strolled past the water tank, I noticed that the cap had not been placed on tightly, and water was gushing out and soaking the ground. I quickly tightened the cover and went in to tell everybody that we somehow had water. They were all elated! We could shower, flush the toilets, and wash clothes. What a wonderful blessing, we all thought, that the refill day had somehow been moved to Monday instead of Thursday.

At 10:00 a.m., the brothers and sisters began arriving for the morning lesson, and when they walked past the kitchen window, they were shocked to see us washing clothes and that everyone was freshly showered. Several of them pulled me aside and reminded me of the water situation. I could tell that they thought we had been careless. I explained to them that we had received water last night and that our tank was full.

"That's impossible," one of the brothers said. "I live in the same zone as the church, and I did not get water last night." We immediately visited some of the homes of our neighbors near the church to see if somehow our brother's house had been skipped the previous night. We discovered that no one else in our zone had received water.

All I could think about after this miracle was the comparison that is often made between Jesus and a spring of water. He told the woman at the well that he could offer her *living* water—a drink that meant she would never be thirsty again. Many people drink alcohol because it helps them forget their problems. Why not seek after a drink that can truly *solve* your problems? This drink exists, and there is an endless supply. Sunday isn't the only day that you can fill your tank with this God-water. It's available any time, and its life-changing power can never be diluted.

FINDING PURPOSE

Now when he came nigh to the gate of the city,
behold, there was a dead man carried out, the
only son of his mother, and she was a widow: and
much people of the city was with her. And when
the Lord saw her, he had compassion on her,
and said unto her, Weep not. And he came and
touched the bier: and they that bare him stood
still. And he said, Young man, I say unto thee' Arise.
And he that was dead sat up, and began to speak.
And he delivered him to his mother.

—Luke 7:12-14

Raising the dead was not a problem for Christ. He
demonstrated this power several times in the New
Testament and gave the same power to the disciples
and the prophets before them. We read the story of Paul
raising up Eutychus after his fall from the window as well
as the accounts of Elisha and Elijah. Given these examples,
today's ministers should expect to perform the same.

One evening, I was called to the Anaheim General
Hospital to pray for a young woman. The first thing I did was
telephone the ladies' prayer group at church for support.
They promised to begin praying immediately, as the
circumstances were grave.

This young lady was a recovering alcoholic who had
been sober for several years. The evening before, she went to
a party and tried something that caused her to go into shock

and placed her in a coma. When I arrived at her room, I saw the doctor standing with three of her friends.

Her boyfriend was weeping because, as I later learned, he felt responsible for taking her to the party where the substances were made available.

Immediately the doctor asked me if I was family. I asked, "Why?"

The doctor explained that he had to place the young lady on life support, but she was clinically dead. The test results showed that her brain was not emitting any activity, but under California law, he could not remove her from support without an immediate family member's approval.

That is when it happened. The words that came out of my mouth were not mine; they were the words of Christ. I said, "She is not dead. She is sleeping."

The doctor laughed weakly and shrugged his shoulders. I walked over to the motionless girl, and I felt an overwhelming wave of compassion for her. I poured the blessed oil on her head and began to pray. As I was praying, she sat up and then lay back down. Everyone got excited except the doctor. He flatly stated that this was normal when someone dies. He said something about how draining fluids can cause the muscles to contract.

I responded, "God has restored her spirit. She will go to a step down unit tomorrow and leave this hospital under her own strength on Friday."

The doctor laughed heartily that time and shook his head. I wonder what was going through that doctor's mind when she walked out of that hospital the following Friday.

. . . .

I know that God extended that young girl's life for a reason. God has a purpose for each one of us, and I have seen Him heal people's illnesses so they could live long enough to fulfill their purpose. For example, the apostle Paul was told by Christ to go to Rome and give his testimony. This was the purpose Jesus set in front of him. On his way to Rome, Paul was arrested and tried by three government officials. A group of forty men took an oath to kill Paul, he was shipwrecked, and then a poisonous snake bit him. But none of these things could prevail against God's commandment. Paul went to Rome and gave his testimony. God extended Paul's life so that he could do what Christ had asked him to do. If our purpose is so important that God is willing to do miracles so we can live long enough to accomplish it, our top priority should be seeking out our spiritual purpose and then working to achieve it.

Caryl and I were going to Spokane, Washington to visit a lady who had an eighty-five-acre piece of land for sale. On it were a home, apple orchards, and a trout hatchery. At the time, we were living in Los Angeles. Moving to Spokane sounded like a great way of life, and we were going to see the property with the hope of one day making it our retirement home.

I took a week off of work. Caryl and I flew to Seattle and then drove to Hayden Lake, Idaho, where we would meet a couple named Patsy and David, who told me about the property and would also take us to see it. As we started driving east from Seattle, the Spirit of God spoke to me and told me to fast.

Fast? I thought with dismay. *I am taking my first real vacation in years, and I want to stop at a great restaurant in Snoqualmie and watch the salmon swim upstream and . . .*

It was useless. God said to fast, so I fasted. I've learned to obey God, no matter how inconvenient it feels at the time or how nonsensical it may seem. Caryl fasted and prayed with me as I drove across Washington State. We arrived at Hayden Lake that evening, where we met Patsy and David. Immediately after the introductions, David said that we needed to go to the hospital and pray for a friend of his named Lydia, who was dying of cancer.

It seemed that David's sister had told him I was an ordained minister, and he urgently felt that he should take me to the hospital. When we got there, the intensive care unit was uncharacteristically bustling and very noisy. With her body full of cancerous tumors, Lydia, weighing in at seventy-eight pounds, had two to three days to live, according to the doctors. *That's okay,* I thought to myself. *A hopeless situation is a great place to start.*

The commotion was distracting, and I asked if we could close the door for some privacy and peace. After clicking the door into place, I looked at Lydia and asked her if she believed in Jesus. She acknowledged that she did, and I started telling her stories about all the wonderful things that He did when He was on earth. As I did, the spirit of peace came into the room, and I told her a story that Brother Joe Lovalvo had told me.

There was a sister in Windsor, Canada who had a tumor between her eyes. The Windsor church fasted and prayed for her, and Brother Joe anointed her. The next day, on the way to the doctor, she sneezed, and to her surprise, the tumor flew into her handkerchief. It looked like a dried raisin. I told Lydia that if she believed, God would cauterize her tumors and extend her life.

Patsy, David, and Caryl held hands with Lydia as I walked around to the back of the hospital bed to anoint her head with oil. As I began to pray, I felt electricity begin to flow through my hands. The harder I prayed, the more powerful the electricity became. After praying for some time, I said, "Lydia, God is doing something marvelous within you. I am going to stop praying, but I will leave my hands on your head as He continues to work."

For a moment, I opened my eyes and saw that David, Patsy, and Caryl had their arms stretched upward to the point of almost lifting Lydia out of the bed. I thought this was interesting, because I had never seen my wife raise her hands during prayer.

As the power started to dissipate, I closed my prayers and stated, "Lydia, God has extended your life so that you can fulfill your purpose."

We left the hospital, and I asked Caryl why she had lifted her hands like that. She exclaimed, "I couldn't help it. As you started to pray, electricity began coursing through my hands and arms. They went up involuntarily."

Lydia did get better. She completed three important things in her life. First, she cared for her ill husband until he died. Second, she designed a collapsible walker. And third, she wrote a book on caring for the terminally ill. She fulfilled her purpose.

But the story doesn't end there. Patsy and David asked us to stay at their home rather than go to a hotel. After some discussion, we felt comfortable saying yes. When we got there, Patsy served us hot tea and warm homemade bread while we sat and talked.

That is when Patsy began telling us her story. Her first husband was killed in an accident. Later, her twelve-year-old son was killed in another accident. Consumed by depression, she had turned to drugs. She had even considered suicide at one point.

Years went by, and she remarried, but the pain remained. She said that about six weeks prior to that night, she was sitting in church with her current husband, listening to the sermon. She said that all of a sudden, she found herself standing in front of a lake next to a man who told her, "Patsy, if you want to serve me, you must be baptized."

"I don't want to be baptized," she responded.

He replied, "You must be baptized to serve me."

She said she reentered her body and finished listening to the sermon. When the service ended, she made a beeline for the minister and asked point-blank to be baptized. He replied that baptism was not necessary any longer. Confused, she went home and prayed. She received an answer immediately. A voice spoke to her and said, "I will send one to baptize you."

She waited several weeks. On the evening I entered their little store and spoke to her husband, David, about the property, she said that the voice spoke to her again and said, "This is the man that I have sent to baptize you."

After I heard this, I felt the spirit of God's confirmation. We baptized Patsy in Hayden Lake the next day. I served her communion, and the Lord did the rest. Patsy went on to full recovery, and she and her husband eventually adopted a son. She was truly born again. Christ gave her back her life so that she could fulfill her purpose.

MESSAGE IN THE MIRACLE

And when they were come to the multitude, there
came to him a certain man, kneeling down to him,
and saying, Lord, have mercy on my son: for he is
lunatick, and sore vexed: for ofttimes he falleth
into the fire, and oft into the water. And I brought
him to thy disciples, and they could not cure
him. Then Jesus answered and said, O faithless
and perverse generation, how long shall I be
with you? How long shall I suffer you? Bring him
hither to me. And Jesus rebuked the devil; and
he departed out of him: and the child was cured
from that very hour. Then came the disciples to
Jesus apart, and said, Why could not we cast him
out? And Jesus said unto them, Because of your
unbelief: for verily I say unto you, If ye have faith
as a grain of mustard seed, ye shall say unto this
mountain, Remove hence to yonder place; and
it shall remove; and nothing shall be impossible
unto you. Howbeit this kind goeth not out but by
prayer and fasting.

—Matthew 17:14-21

I have never fasted for more than three days straight.
Reading about how Jesus, Moses, and others fasted for
forty days boggles my mind. Even though my efforts
have not been as tremendous, the results of my fasts have
always been wondrous. The timing has to be right, and
the environment must be conducive to fasting, study, and
prayer. I always had to be prepared to tune out worldly

interferences and focus on the spiritual. I have fasted at work whenever special needs would arise at midday. I would take my lunchtime and find a place to pray. I believe God sees the intent of our hearts, understands the necessities of our lives, and honors our efforts.

I had just finished a period of fasting before a business trip took me to Tampa, Florida, where the church had a mission. I attended the Wednesday evening service, and as is the custom with visiting ministry, I was asked to take the lead and speak to the congregation. I used Matthew 17 as the foundation of my talk.

When I finished, several people came up for prayer. One man walked up with his son, who appeared to be about seven or eight years old. This man was not a member of the church but had been visiting for a few months. His heart was touched by the sermon, and he asked if I could pray for his son. I asked him what the problem was. He replied that his son was epileptic.

As the young man sat in the chair, my mind thought of how the disciples had struggled because they were not able to heal the man's son. I knew that, without knowing it, I had prepared myself for this moment. God had prepared me, and He had inspired me with a message that had prompted this man to ask a healing upon his son. This was serious. I knelt first and offered my heart to God, asking Him to fill me with His Spirit and power. Then I stood, anointed the child with oil, laid my hands on his head, and prayed.

One evening, about two weeks later, I saw that I had a message on my home answering machine. When I played it,

I heard, "Hello, Brother John. I don't know if you remember me, but I met you at the church in Tampa a couple of weeks ago. My name is Kevin. After your sermon, I brought my son up for prayer. He has been treated for epilepsy for several years. Last week, we went to the doctor for his regular visit, and the doctor was very confused. He said that my son doesn't have epilepsy any longer. I know he was healed when you prayed for him, so I wanted to say thank you."

I called Kevin back, and we both rejoiced as he told me the details of his son's examination. I then felt compelled to ask him, "Kevin, what is the message to *you* in this miracle?"

Kevin replied, "I want to serve Jesus Christ. I want to be baptized."

Kevin is now an ordained minister in The Church of Jesus Christ, and he plays an active role in bringing the gospel to the mission field.

LITTLE BENNIE

"And his disciples asked him, saying, Master, who did sin, this man, or his parents, that he was born blind? Jesus answered, Neither hath this man sinned, nor his parents: but that the works of God should be made manifest in him."

—John 9:2-3

God often performs miracles in order to aid people through the conversion process. When people see the undeniable power of God, they have no choice but to come to grips with the fact that He exists. They have no choice but to *make a choice*—either believe the miracle and believe that Jesus performed it or deny the miracle and reject the grace of Christ. If God didn't shake people up with miracles, most of us would just spend our whole lives never facing the question of whether God exists. But once we witness a miracle, we no longer have that option.

God's miracles come in all forms, but none have the impact that physical healings have. The New Testament is full of stories in which Christ and the apostles performed all types of healings. Since Jesus Christ is the same yesterday, today, and forever, why shouldn't we see miracles today? If my stories haven't already spoken for themselves, I will say clearly and unequivocally that miracles *do* happen.

My friend, Bob, and I were doing missionary work on the western slope of the Colorado Rockies. The community that God sent me to was very quaint and rather earthy.

These folks were organic farmers for the most part, and they preferred bartering with each other rather than buying and selling. I had made several trips there, and while I had been well received, I knew that at the rate things were going, it was going to take a long time to convert these practical but skeptical people.

One day, I heard about a little boy who was in nursing home in town who everyone knew as Little Bennie. The boy had been playing behind his father's truck in the driveway and been run over. His neck had been broken, and the doctors in Denver said that he would never move again. Their recommendation was to take him off life support and allow him to die. But Little Bennie had a believing grandmother, and she refused to have the life support turned off. Instead, she placed him in this little nursing home in the western Rockies, awaiting God to move his hand.

Bennie was eight years old, and he had lain in the same position for three years. Therapists exercised his muscles, and nurses talked to him every day, but for three years, there was never a movement or a response from Little Bennie.

I decided to go see this child in the nursing home, and Bob came along with me.

Standing over Bennie's bed, I noticed that his body had atrophied. His adult teeth had not come in, and his body was shapeless under the wrinkled white bed sheets. Compassion filled my soul for this child. I anointed Bennie and poured out my heart to Christ for his healing, knowing that Jesus had more compassion for Bennie than I could ever fathom. We left the nursing home and continued visiting and inviting the whole town to attend our evening service at the Grange Hall.

The meeting went well that evening, and the response from the farmers was wonderful. They sang with enthusiasm and listened attentively. Several gave their testimonies, and we made plans to meet again the next day. But I could not get my mind off Little Bennie.

Even after we got back to the hotel, I was still plagued with questions. *Why has not God healed him?* I thought. *Why didn't He demonstrate His power and show these people that He is alive?* Knowing that miracles shake people up and cause them to consider the existence of God, I believed that a miracle was exactly what the town needed to see.

Bob saw that I was discouraged, and he asked why. I told him that I was disappointed that God had not healed Little Bennie. Bob suggested that we pray. We both got on our knees, and he offered prayer first. Then as I began to pray, the Spirit of God fell on me powerfully, and I asked Jesus to go to the nursing home and heal Little Bennie. I told him that I did not want any honor or glory for myself and that it all belonged to Him.

We awoke early the next day for the Sunday service. We were busy getting ready when someone knocked at our door. When I opened it, I was greeted by a cowboy standing in front of me with his hat in his hand. He said that he, his wife, and his daughter were in the room next door and that they heard us praying the previous night. He and his family felt such urgency in our voices that they got on their knees and joined us.

"I'm sorry for praying so loudly," I began sheepishly.

"Don't!" he interrupted, and then humbly asked, "Could you pray for *me?*"

"Sure. What do you need prayer for?"

"I need work," he admitted.

"Come on in," I said. The man entered and sat on the corner of the hotel bed. I prayed that God would provide work for this man who had assisted me with my prayers the previous evening. I became even more convinced that this town needed to see miracles.

After the Sunday meeting, Bob and I drove the eighteen hours back to California and returned to our normal routine. About a week later, I received a letter from one of the older ladies I had met in Colorado. She was *so* excited, she wrote, because everyone in town was talking about Little Bennie. He had started to move and make sounds. With each passing day, he was becoming more responsive. *Incredible,* I thought as I got on my knees and thanked and praised God for His goodness. I couldn't wait to make my next trip there. I called Bob, and we made plans to go back in early September.

Upon arrival, we went straight to the nursing home. I guess I expected to see Little Bennie running around, playing ball and talking with the other children, but he wasn't. The nurse wakened him, and it took quite a while before he was responsive and moving. The sounds coming out of his mouth were guttural, and his atrophied body struggled to perform even the smallest commands from his nervous system.

I was disappointed. I anticipated seeing him in much better shape. Why hadn't the Lord given Little Bennie an instant healing like I had seen Him do for so many others I had known? It was what the town needed. After a few torturous moments of asking why, I realized that the Lord knew what He was doing. He was fully capable of healing this young boy, and if He chose not to, then there was a good reason for it. I could believe this and continue trusting the Lord who had done so much for me, or—what other choice was there? Give up my faith? Decide that God wasn't really in control? Despair? No, that way of thinking was not an option.

I refocused my mind. I realized that while Little Bennie was not instantly healed, he was on the road to recovery. That was something to praise God for. I acknowledged that it would take time and tremendous effort for his muscles to develop and his nerves to be fully functional again. I began to realize that sometimes God, instead of answering us right away with a faith-building miracle, asks us to trust Him through a process.

While I still felt somewhat let down, Bob was so excited that he asked the nurse if we could take Bennie outside for a walk. The nurse was very pleased, and she quickly bundled him up and strapped him safely in a wheelchair. It was a beautiful fall day in the mountains. The sky was bright blue, and the aspen leaves had changed to every warm shade of orange and yellow. It created a scene that was breathtaking no matter where we looked. But Bennie could not see them; he had not opened his eyes in three years.

After walking for a few minutes, Bob felt to sing to Bennie. He positioned himself on his knees in front of

Bennie's wheelchair and cupped Bennie's little atrophied hands in his own large paws. He began with his favorite hymn:

> Amazing grace how sweet the sound
> That saved a wretch like me,
> I once was lost but now I'm found,
> Was blind but now I see.

Amazing Grace John Newton

When Bob sang the words "was blind but now I see," Bennie's eyelids began to part so that a tiny crack appeared. This crack widened until the whites of Bennie's eyes could be seen all around the pupil. He began turning his head from side to side in order to behold the vista. We heard sounds coming from his throat that sounded like *oohs* and *aahs*. Bennie was seeing for the first time in three years.

Bob and I were so excited and filled with the Spirit from our afternoon with Bennie that we conducted a wonderful meeting that night. The singing, preaching, and testimonies glorified God, and we departed on a high note.

As we left the hall, we had to travel down a very dark, narrow country road in order to get back to our hotel. I paused at a stop sign, and to my surprise, standing to my left about two feet from the window of my car was the most beautiful deer that I had ever seen. His rack was made up of fourteen points, and they were in perfect symmetry—seven on each side. He didn't move, and I stared into his watery eyes for several minutes. *How majestic and regal,* I thought to myself.

After a few minutes of admiring this incredible animal, I pulled away from the stop sign and continued on my way. As I did, the Spirit of God fell on me, and I heard the following: "You were like Little Bennie. You had eyes but could not see. You had ears but could not hear, and you had a mouth that could not speak. It was not until you were born again that you became the creature that I intend you to be—like the deer."

I began to weep as the realization crashed over me. I remembered the man I was before my conversion. I remembered all the things that happened to transform me into the person I had grown to be. I realized that God had been transforming me. The new man I had become—even though I was still a work in progress—was truly a miracle. I already knew all this, but it was the first time I fully understood what it meant.

Then I remembered that, like Little Bennie, my life had also been a process, not an instant healing. The decision to be baptized took about six weeks, and that process had just been the beginning of my spiritual growth. It wasn't an immediate conversion. I was still being converted each day in deeper and more meaningful ways. If I remained open to it, every day would become a chance to emulate Christ a little better. When I allow this, I can become more like my true self—shedding the exteriors we all build up so we can hide behind them—and become the person I was intended to be.

We are all on this journey, and as we press along, we catch sublime moments when we get glimpses of the heavenly. We *ooh* and *aah* like Bennie at the sight, only to later realize that it was always there for us to see. All we have to do is open our eyes. Like our true selves, *we* have always been there. It takes Christ to introduce us to ourselves. Michaelangelo, when asked how he carved the statue of David, replied, "The perfect David was always in the block of marble. I just had to chip away that which wasn't him." Our true self exists and has always been inside us. Christ helps us chip away at those things that are not us. He never gives up on us, like Bennie's doctors had. He will always be with us, until the end.

> "Go ye therefore, and teach all nations, baptizing
> them in the name of the Father, and of the Son,
> and of the Holy Ghost: Teaching them to observe
> all things whatsoever I have commanded you:
> and, lo, I am with you always, even unto the end of
> the world. Amen." (Matthew 28:19-20)

REFUSING TO BELIEVE

And as he entered into a certain village, there met
him ten men that were lepers, which stood afar
off. And they lifted up their voices, and said, Jesus,
Master, have mercy on us. And when he saw them,
he said unto them, Go shew yourselves unto the
priests. And it came to pass, that, as they went,
they were cleansed. And one of them, when he
saw that he was healed, turned back, and with
a loud voice glorified God, And fell down on his
face at his feet, giving him thanks: and he was a
Samaritan. And Jesus answering said, Were there
not ten cleansed? but where are the nine?

—Luke 17:12-17

God's Spirit and salvation are available to everyone,
but the road that leads to this realization is
encumbered with many versions of the same
loathsome obstacle: self. What the self wants is an obstacle:
self-pity, self-importance, and the nastiest of all, self-love.
Unfortunate as it may be, it often takes a crisis to bring
about change in our lives and start us down the path of
self-discovery (a good self). That is what happened to me
when I suddenly became dissatisfied with my life for no
apparent reason. I will be eternally grateful that I chose to
accept Christ as the solution for my life's emptiness; however,
I have seen many who, even after experiencing miracles,
choose not to engage in the process of spiritual growth.

Over the last twenty years, I have had a number of colleagues who have asked me to pray for ailments that ran the gamut from cancer to hepatitis to nervous disorders. One such case occurred at a convention I was attending with a coworker in New Orleans. I heard a knock on my hotel room door one evening, and I was surprised to see my coworker on the other side of it. I had shared my convictions with him in the past, and he confided to me that he had cancer. It had spread to the point where he was somehow bleeding internally. I offered a simple prayer for him.

Several years later at a dinner function, this same coworker told my wife that he had been healed of cancer through that prayer I had offered so long ago. Caryl asked him why he had never shared that with me before, and he responded, "Oh, John would have probably expected me to go to church or something."

Isn't it strange that people would rather not get close to God—even when He has performed miracles to lengthen their lives? They would rather deny that He had done anything special for them. No matter how vigorously we try to be masters of our own lives, we are going to eventually have to acknowledge Christ as God and Lord. Whether that time comes in this life or in the next, it will come—surely enough.

> "That at the name of Jesus every knee should bow, of things in heaven, and things in earth, and things under the earth." (Phillipians 2:10)

When I was preaching in that little town in the western Rockies where I met Little Bennie, I encountered a man named Ken who regularly ridiculed me and the subject of my sermons. He claimed to be an atheist. Sometimes Ken would attend my meetings, and then he would often ask me to have a cup of coffee the next day, always trying to stir me up into a debate. He would say things like, "Only a fool would believe all that rubbish" and "In the face of science, the Bible's stories are like nursery rhymes." After I left the little city, he usually used his column in the local newspaper to blast me.

Each time I visited this town, I always had coffee with him. Although I will not argue about the gospel, I am willing to discuss it with anybody. *Besides,* I thought to myself, *if he converts, many might follow.*

During one of my trips, Ken didn't show up at any of the meetings. I asked about him, and someone told me that he had been diagnosed with congestive heart failure. He was on oxygen and unable to leave the house much anymore. So I went to visit him. Caryl; my traveling partner, Bob; and Bob's wife, Sandy, were with me. I knew that Ken would never allow me to pray for him, but I had another idea. Ken loved music, and Bob loved to sing. Bob's favorite hymn is, of course, "Amazing Grace." When we finished our visit, I asked Ken if he would like to hear our little quartet sing a song. Before he could respond, we all started singing "Amazing Grace." By the time we got to that last verse, Ken was trembling.

> When we've been there ten thousand years
> Bright shining as the sun
> We've no less days to sing God's praise
> Than when we first begun.

Ken was holding back tears while gripping his walker, trying to maintain composure. We left not knowing if we would see Ken again. We almost didn't. Apparently, Ken was rushed to the hospital with heart failure shortly after our visit with him. His daughter told me that he flatlined three times, and each time, the doctors were able to bring him back using the defibrillator. She said, "Each time he started to slip away, he began crying out for help. He cried, 'Help me! Help me; I need John. Somebody get John.'"

At first, his family didn't know whom Ken wanted them to get—I was only a visitor in that town—but they eventually realized that Ken was calling for the traveling preacher. When I talked to Ken later about this experience, he told me, "When I felt my spirit descending into hell, I realized that I had been wrong. For years, I had denied the truth. I knew what you told me was true. That's why I cried out for you to help me."

After Ken recovered, he was a different man. The next time I saw him was on a beautiful spring Sunday. Ken's attitude seemed to match the fresh spring flowers and new buds on the trees. He was humble, and he lovingly held his wife's hand as they walked together—to church.

Every soul is important to God—even souls who mock and deny Him, like Ken. He had taken measures to inhibit people from accepting Christ, but that didn't stop Christ from accepting him. The Holy Spirit worked on him until the last possible minute to bring him salvation.

. . . .

As you read these stories, my prayer is that your spirit has been encouraged, strengthened, and nourished by knowing that the Holy Spirit is alive and working in people's lives. I urge you to meditate on the events in your life where the Lord has intervened—especially the times that seemed the most heartbreaking and hopeless. Our greatest periods of inner growth often take place during periods of greatest trial. Paul knew this when he wrote,

> "And he said unto me, My grace is sufficient for thee: for my strength is made perfect in weakness. Most gladly therefore will I rather glory in my infirmities, that the power of Christ may rest upon me" (2 Corinthians 12:9).

Paul knew what it meant to be strongest at the point of greatest weakness. When he was imprisoned, beaten, stoned, or poisoned, these were the times when God's power was manifested in such a way that it couldn't be denied by those who witnessed it. Unfortunately, many are unwilling to give themselves over to their Creator. We want to live life our way and on our own terms. When we do this, we are unable to use our greatest strength, our inner being—the part of us that is not bound by the physical laws of this earth but freed by the spiritual law of love.

There is no magic formula that works for everyone. As you have read, Christ will meet you in a hospital room, a flying car, a bus station, or the quietness of your own heart. Whether your life is just beginning or coming to an end, Christ's forgiveness and love are available to all.

FINAL JOURNEY

I would be remiss not to share this last story with you, as it involves the last missionary trip of my mentor and spiritual father, Brother Joseph Lovalvo. For more than fifteen years, he mentored me in my spiritual walk, but I never had the opportunity to share a missionary trip with him. However, about two years before he died, I received a call that his two daughters and niece were going to take him back to Sicily to visit the place of his birth. They asked if I was going to be in Italy for the annual conference, and if so, whether they could attend with Brother Joe. "Of course," I responded. What an honor it would be for the brothers and sisters to meet and hear this ninety-four-year-old preach the gospel in his native tongue.

About three weeks before the conference, our eighty-two-year-old Sister Immacolata, the spiritual impetus for the church in Sardinia, had a stroke, fell, and broke three vertebrae. The doctors in the hospital in *Provincio di Nuoro* said that she had reached the end and sent her home to die.

One morning, shortly after Immacolata had the stroke, I received a call from one of her granddaughters. Marta was excited and said that her grandmother had had a vision that morning where she saw me standing at the bottom of her bed, praying for her. She wondered what this meant. I assured Marta that I was praying for her grandmother and that possibly God was just comforting her grandmother with a knowledge that we loved her and were lifting her up in prayer.

The next day, I received a second call from Marta. This time, she related another vision that her grandmother had where there were two of us at her bedside—me and an older man whom she did not recognize.

Upon arrival in Sardinia, we went immediately to see Sister Immacolata. Bedbound, in great pain, and unable to move her left side, she lay staring blankly at me. Of course, I anointed her and prayed for a complete recovery.

The next day, Brother Joe arrived, and we sat and talked about the conference. He asked what we were going to do that evening, and I explained to him that it was customary to visit the elderly and sick. I had expected him to want to relax and catch up on some rest; after all, he was nine hours ahead in that time zone, and he was ninety-four years old. That was not to be the case—I picked him up at 9:00, and our first stop was to see Immacolata.

When we arrived at the apartment complex, I thought how foolish I was. Her flat was on the third floor, and there were no elevators—only twenty-seven high marble steps. Brother Joe couldn't possibly make it to the top even with the aid of his cane. At the bottom of the steps, I began to apologize for bringing him there. He immediately turned, wacked me with his cane, and laughingly said, "I am not dead yet!"

Up we went, with me trailing behind, contemplating how I would explain to the church that Brother Joe died on my watch climbing these steps.

Once we entered the flat, Joe pointed to me and said, "Let's kneel and pray, John, and ask God for His healing power."

As we stood, I handed Brother Joe the little bottle of blessed oil that I carry. He didn't have to bend too far, as he was already bent over from age; he just set his cane down and applied the oil to Immacolata's head. He laid hands on her and began to pray for a healing. When Joe was finished, the funniest thing I ever saw happened. Sister Immacolata took her good right arm, threw it around Joe's neck, and pulled him closer so that she could kiss him—not once, but with dozens of little smooches. I had never seen anything like this, and while she was doing so, Joe turned to me and said, "John, this sister was really blessed by that prayer. What do you think?"

We laughed and knew that he was the older man in her vision and that something wonderful had just happened.

What do you think? The next day, with the use of a walker, Sister Immacolata made her way into the kitchen for dinner, and two weeks later, she walked into church under her own strength without any aids. As she entered the sanctuary, she lifted her hands in the air to give thanks to the living God. Witnesses said that they could feel the building shaking.

Once again, Joe was teaching me—just as he had at his home in Modesto. No matter what the situation may look like to the human eye—no matter how old, desperate, or improbable it may look—*nothing* is impossible to the living God.

CONCLUSION

Therefore I say unto you, Take no thought for your
life, what ye shall eat, or what ye shall drink; nor
yet for your body, what ye shall put on. Is not the
life more than meat, and the body than raiment?
Behold the fowls of the air: for they sow not,
neither do they reap, nor gather into barns; yet
your heavenly Father feedeth them. Are ye not
much better than they?

—Matthew 6:25-26

The fact of the matter is that there is no conclusion
with God. He is eternal, without beginning or end.
We are the ones who need time, but with God, there
is no such thing. He is in the past, present, and future. He is
the great *I am*. We, on the other hand, are only in the present.
There is nothing we can do about the past, nor is our future
secure. Only when we operate in the present can we operate
in sync with the Lord and access His matchless power.

Since the completion of this book, I have already
experienced several more instances of God's grace and
abundant power while in His service. My hope is that you
have been inspired to try the same. As you have read, your
personal journey starts with a simple desire. The steps follow
a sequence of wanting to know more and studying the
Scriptures, seeking deeper understanding and meditating,
testing and experimenting through prayer, and going as
far as you can go—fasting. Through this process, God will
change you as He sees fit. By doing these things, you place

yourself on the potter's wheel, and He will begin molding and shaping who you are now into the real you—the you He intended you to be. This process is not without pain, discomfort, or sorrow, but the rewards far outweigh any temporary sadness.

When I have the privilege of telling of these experiences in person, people often listen in amazement. They feel the Holy Spirit confirming the truth of my words. Many times, they say, "John, you are special. Not all of us have these gifts." Let me be perfectly clear—God wants to work through you as well. He doesn't consider some people more worthy than others. He loves us all equally, and He is willing to pour out a blessing upon anyone who earnestly seeks.

God sent His only Son into the world to die for our sins so that we can enter heaven after our lives are over. He wants every human being on earth to hear this good news, and if you have a desire to introduce this joyful message to others, ask the Lord to help you. He will bless you with the tools you need to reach people for Him. Sometimes He will inspire your mouth to speak words of enlightenment. Sometimes He will inspire your heart to pray without a shred of doubt. Sometimes He will fill a hopeless situation with His undeniable power, and miracles will occur. He will do whatever it takes for the good news to click in someone's heart and mind. I pray that you have a desire to be part of whatever it takes to tell others that God loves them!

> "For God so loved the world, that he gave his only begotten Son, that whosoever believeth in him should not perish, but have everlasting life." (John 3:16)